TAKING THE LONG WAY HOME

A PEACE CORPS MEMOIR OF BRAZIL

ANNE SPRY

Flint Hills Publishing

Praise for Taking the Long Way Home...

"Anne Spry vividly captures the tensions of a Peace Corps Volunteer navigating rural Brazilian life in the early 1970s in the service of community development. She clearly chronicles the language and cultural challenges, the essential interpersonal relationships amid personal agendas, accommodating both government and religious priorities, persevering through setbacks and misunderstandings, and more. The author's three-year assignment is a testament to her indefatigable persistence to problem solve and adapt while respecting the people in order to positively influence the quality of their lives."

–Ken Weaver, Peace Corps Volunteer, 1973, Philippines, rural public health; professor emeritus of psychology, Emporia State University

"Come along on Anne Spry's literal and emotional journey as a 1970s' Midwest anti-war activist to (in her words) "do-gooder" Peace Corps volunteer on the poor rural sugar plantations of Brazil. What she learns and how she grows as a woman and citizen of the world will fill you with admiration for this wise and talented writer."

–Ruth Maus, author of Lunacy And Acts of God

"Every Peace Corps volunteer's story is unique to them. What they bring from their lived experiences, the culture and country where they serve, and the obstacles they face in their assignment all shape their stories. Anne Spry shares this all in her recounting of Brazil in the early 1970's. I have similar memories from my time in Romania in the late 1990s. Arrogant, powerful men in a patriarchal society, desperate mothers and young girls struggling to provide every-day needs, and the challenges and beauty of the unfamiliar landscape collide against the optimistic idealism brought by the volunteer. All of us who served have been forever changed by the Peace Corps experience."

–Linda Tuller, small business development volunteer, Romania, 1996-98; retired from banking and sales

"I've known Anne for 40 years. She gave me a start in journalism and gave me the guts to go for a lengthy career in newspapers. This memoir of Anne's from her days at the University of Missouri and time in the Peace Corps, reads like a novel about embracing an idealistic youth, awakenings and accepting (reluctantly?) the world as it is. This book is about joyful hellos and tearful goodbyes. It's about relationships, both cherished and strained. It's about finding yourself and then losing yourself in your work. It's about new beginnings, over and over again. Finally, it's about baring your soul, coming to terms with yourself and finding healing through the written word. The author takes you through twists and turns navigated in the Civil Rights/Vietnam era that polarized the U.S. in the 1960s and 70s. Finally, it's about where you are, where you've been and the comfort you've found just being who you are."

–*Dennis Cox, retired newspaper editor, local historian, and author of* **Hamilton, Missouri: A Place of Pride and Progress**

Taking the Long Way Home – A Peace Corps
Memoir of Brazil© 2025 by Anne Spry

Cover Design by Amy Albright

Author Photograph by Timeless Portraits

Flint Hills Publishing

Topeka, Kansas
Tucson, Arizona
www.flinthillspublishing.com

Printed in the U.S.A.

Paperback Book ISBN: 978-1-966323-28-0
Electronic Book ISBN: 978-1-966323-29-7
Hardcover Book ISBN: 978-1-966323-30-3

Library of Congress Control Number: 2025914580

To Michael

When I met Brazilian children for the first time, I was pleased and surprised when they held their hands out to me and asked, "Bless me, Auntie." I was expected to respond by placing my hand on their heads and saying, "Deus te abençoi."

When you asked me to write the story of the days your dad and I were in the Peace Corps, I tried to take the easy way out and transcribe my journals. You would not accept that. You wanted it to read like a novel. By making that request, you heaped blessings on my own head.

Deus te abençoi, meu filho.

CONTENTS

Map of Brazil

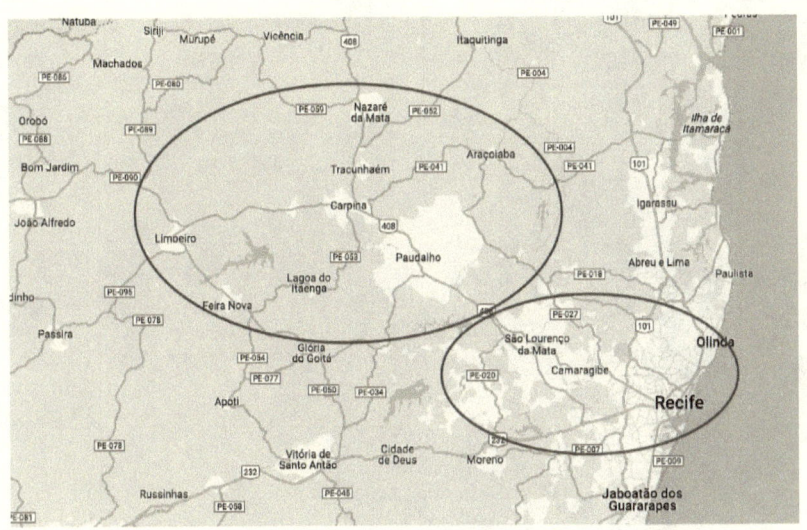

Places we worked and traveled.

FOREWORD

DR. WALT MENNINGER

I read *Taking the Long Way Home* from the perspective of having served as a psychiatrist in the Peace Corps' Washington, D.C. office in only the second year of the agency's existence. I worked with volunteers in both the initial selection phase and the completion of service debriefings at the end of their tours. In studying the responses to questionnaires given to 1,000 returning volunteers, we noticed predictable patterns in adapting to a new situation. We began to call this pattern the Morale Curve.

Part of the curve includes a step called "the crisis of engagement." I immediately identified author Anne Spry's crisis of engagement when she writes, "Just six months into our assignment in Brazil, and I am questioning everything. Why are we here? How can we ever hope to accomplish any good in this place when we have to battle three centuries of entrenched poverty and misery?"

This captivating memoir demonstrates how our lives are influenced by the way we traverse our different paths. It's an extraordinary articulation of a maturing-life experience while engaging with a new primitive world as a Peace Corps volunteer. *Taking the Long Way Home* reflects energy, enthusiasm, idealism, and resilience.

Spry's work, and any Peace Corps memoir, is a testament to the role individuals can play in person-to-person diplomacy and interactions in this fractured world. It recalls my memory of how the ideals of the organization were captured so beautifully in 1964 by Thanat Khoman, Foreign Minister of Thailand, when he called the Peace Corps one of the most important ideas in recent times. He said that such ideas and ideals are the secret of the greatness and might of the United States, "…which is not imposing or crushing people, but is filled with the hope of future goodwill and understanding."

I fear that the future and image of the Peace Corps has been imperiled by recent budget cuts and the decimation of its D.C. staff. However, I've long felt that the individual volunteers were the chief beneficiaries of the experiences and relationships they developed overseas. Author Spry is now much richer in spirit and knowledge of life from her time in Brazil. And so is anyone who reads this book.

Dr. Walt Menninger
Former President and CEO The Menninger Clinic
August, 2025

BROKEN HOMES, BROKEN HEART

Home is where the heart is, or so the poets say.

As I sang the opening strains to a barbershop version of "Somewhere Over the Rainbow" with the Sweet Adelines chorus I belong to, I tried not to feel the emotion behind the words. We were supposed to emote so our music would be more genuine. But home has always been a touchy subject for me. I've had more homes than a military family and they haven't all been happy ones.

My first home in Wakarusa, Kansas was where I learned to exit my crib, talk in full sentences before the age of one, and march in circles around the dining room table chanting, "Poor Anne. No Mommy. No Daddy. No Raisnuts" (my word for raisins). In that first home I learned how to share with my brother by dividing a saltine cracker in pieces, but found myself face-planted on the splintered wood of our front porch by my mother when I tried to keep the biggest piece for myself.

I wish I could have stayed in my second home forever. I loved the knotty pine walls of the upstairs playroom on 45th Street in Topeka, the sweet-smelling hayloft in the barn that held my old nag named Bullet, the boathouse where I taught myself to love music by playing on a mouse-infested piano. That 20-acre place also held the abandoned brooder house I made into a playhouse, shoving out straw and chicken manure and hauling in rusted box springs and wooden box "furniture." It was my make-believe, big people house where I rehearsed adulthood by repeatedly welcoming my five-year-old male playmate home from his "day at work."

My Oklahoma home was a 55-foot Nashua house trailer my mother hauled to Tulsa to keep us safe from a violent man she brought home from a local skating rink after my father died in a truck accident. A flood, poverty, and hunger would soon force our return to rural Kansas to park the trailer in the driveway of my grandparents' home. At least until Mother could find another broken man to whisk us away to live in a post-war crackerbox house in suburban Kansas City.

When Mother had enough of that man's abuse, we found a house in a new sub-division a few miles away, with a new stepfather. There I learned to clean house at age 13 with all the curtains closed to cocoon me safely away from constant chaos and change. I even found comfort and stability in learning to polish Mother's massive silver tea service, the one possession that gave her hope for future prosperity.

Then, for want of a husband who was a good provider, we moved to another crackerbox house in a different suburb, with neighbors who worked at the nearby Richards Gebauer Air Force Base. In that house I had a perfect lilac-colored bedroom with rustling satin-striped drapes. The same room where Mother smashed my new bottle of Emeraude cologne I'd purchased with babysitting money. The same house where my stepfather threw my 16th birthday present at me, disgusted because I had retreated to my best friend's house while the rest of the family went to the lake for the weekend. That house should have been my launchpad into adult life, but we moved to a rented farmhouse the summer before I left for college. My tiny room there was a sun porch, which got converted to a sewing room right after I left for the University of Missouri. When I came home the following summer, I had to string up a curtain across the upstairs bedroom I shared with my younger brother to find any privacy.

I couldn't wait to leave home and get married so I could make a new home for myself. After three years of dorm rooms and a dank summer basement rental in a college town, I got married two days after my 21st birthday and moved into a 55-foot Nashua trailer.

When my new husband and I graduated from the University of Missouri in 1971, both of us with degrees in journalism, we set up temporary homes in Northeast Brazil as Peace Corps volunteers. In this foreign land, where they spoke Portuguese and often had nothing more to eat than rice and beans … in this beautiful country where houses often had dirt floors and hammocks for beds … I learned the importance of having a purpose bigger than ourselves. In Brazil I also began the arduous journey to the home inside my heart and now recognize it as the only safe place to live.

But first, I had to clear out stacks of emotional clutter.

Anne and Dan's passport photos.

PART I: PLACES

NORTHWEST BRAZIL
AND
MIDWEST USA

-1-

HUNGER IN THE JUNGLE
AND IN THE USA

As he aimed a stream of clay-tinged water from the outside spigot at the narrow mouth of a 5-liter can, José Paulo scratched his head in puzzled contemplation. Why did almost everyone on the sugar cane plantation delight in tormenting him? Why did they laugh in his face and behind his back, no matter how serious the subject?

On this humid day in September of 1971, as he started the first of several daily chores, the little bow-legged man slopped water all over himself as he hoisted the heavy container onto his head.

Jesus, Mary. and Joseph! For some reason it seemed especially painful today. Then he grinned at his forgetfulness. The cloth.

He lowered the square aluminum can bearing the logo for Brazilian kerosene onto the ground again. Pulling a soiled piece of muslin out of his back pocket, José formed a circular pad, placed it on his head, then grunted under the strain as he hauled the water back into place. He set off slowly, padding in his splayed bare feet, and soon settled into a swaying gait but managed to keep the can level.

One trip to the American teacher now and two later this morning to the overseer's house. That meant two hills to climb, three times. José needed both hands to balance the water, but one hand was occupied with a crushed straw hat.

"Put the hat on top of the water, no?" Soon the bizarrely-hatted water bearer continued on his path, muttering under his breath in resentment.

"Carrying water is a woman's work. But if God wants me to carry water, I'm not one to argue with the ways of the Lord."

He stumbled along the manure-pocked path by the pond where

Carlos was washing a mule. The geese honked, hissed, and chased José, who retaliated with a kick that nearly landed him in the mud. The only decent goose was that crippled one. It never hissed, just walked sort of catty-corner, like José was doing right now.

The burdened little man struggled up a steep hill made slippery by September rains. Short of breath, he arrived at a whitewashed house surrounded by discarded sugar cane kettles repurposed as flowerpots. José found that strange. What a waste to turn those immense metal containers into a frivolous thing and then plant flowers! His own father had probably stood for hours at this very kettle, in the broiling heat, stirring the extracted syrup from the sugar cane before it was made into *rapadura*, the coarse, tan-colored sugar that all the plantations like Tamataupe de Flores sent out for further processing to nearby *usinas* (larger sugar mills).

José snorted at the sight of a blanket of moss roses spilling out of the kettles. *Can you eat those?* he wondered, gazing at the multitude of colors and their thick, succulent stems. He stood at the hut's back door and cried out, "Oh, the house!" If he had not been using both hands to balance things, he would have clapped as well in the traditional Brazilian greeting. His voice was barely audible above his panting.

"You're here early," said the American woman as she opened the top half of the wooden door.

"*Bom dia*," José smiled weakly. His stomach rumbled at the sights and smells emanating from the kitchen. A coffee pot boiled on the shiny metal stove fueled by a kerosene tank. Papaya, bananas, and sweet bread teased him from the red and white checkered oilcloth that covered a small table.

Oh, to be rich and eat breakfasts like that! He knew the American lady and her husband were rich, even though they pretended to live like the rest of the plantation tenants. After all, they had a Jeep. And they were sometimes even dinner guests at the *casa grande*. The whole plantation was mystified at why this young couple had left their country, where they probably had their own casa grande, to come and live like peasants.

The woman everyone called Dona Ana removed the lid from a waist-high clay water jar. She positioned a cheesecloth over the mouth of the jar to filter out debris and motioned for José to start pouring. His head was now shaking visibly as he shifted the weight downward, managing to empty some of the can's contents onto the cement floor.

Ana stifled a laugh and thought, *Not your usual Brazilian macho man.*

In the first place, he was fair-haired and light-skinned. You didn't see much of that here in Northeast Brazil. Maybe he had some Dutch blood in his ancestry from the days the invaders occupied the state of Pernambuco. But she quickly felt contrite for her muffled laughter as she watched him fill the water jar. His buttonless flour sack shirt gaped open all the way to his waist. She glimpsed an almost hairless chest, yellow, mottled skin, and ribs so prominent she could count them. She quickly averted her gaze to his feet, so caked with layers of mud they appeared to be shoes. She wondered if he even owned a pair of rubber flip-flops, the footwear of choice among all poor Brazilians.

Ana felt sorry for José, a pity that was perhaps stronger than what she felt for every poor person she had encountered so far in this beautiful country. Even his gray eyes suggested weakness. The only thing about José Paulo that made her think he had any character besides weakness was his rambling but often eloquent speech. He spoke each word with narrowed eyes and elaborate gestures of his calloused, caked-dirt-under-fingernails hands. His voice often rose into a soprano that almost squeaked, but other times modulated to a whispered baritone to emphasize the gravity of his subjects. José Paulo took himself seriously, in huge contrast to how most people perceived him.

"Since well early this morning I have been working so hard at my service. And me so hungry," the comic little man told Dona Ana, casting a sideways glance at the table. "Not even a cup of coffee did I have because a drop of coffee we didn't have in the house.

"But I don't complain," he continued his monologue,

11

scratching a head capped with frizzy gray and yellow hair. "No. Because I trust in God in the sky and in his great power and in the grace of all the saints." José then looked heavenward and gave his Creator a beatific smile.

Suddenly Ana remembered she hadn't paid the man who hauled up five liters of water every day and an extra can on Saturdays for the outside shower/privy. The shower was an ingenious bucket with a sprinkler head on the bottom and a shut-off handle on the side. She and her husband Dan usually heated a gallon of water on the stove, added it to another gallon of unheated water, and stood under it once a week to shower, while looking up at the turquoise skies of the *Pernambuco Zona da Mata* (jungle zone). At times Ana imagined she could detect the scent of the Atlantic Ocean that was a little over an hour away as the *urubu* flies from their humble hut and outdoor privy. The ocean drew them frequently to Recife, the state's capital city, where they often met other Peace Corps volunteers and staged spontaneous beach parties.

Ana checked her reverie when she heard José nervously clearing his throat. She left the kitchen to pull two crumpled cruzeiro notes out of her purse, knowing she didn't have to pay him at all. The plantation owner's son-in-law paid him. But she doubted it was much to exist on, since the cane cutters who lived in scattered huts were only paid the equivalent of a dollar a day. A *casa grande* worker like this man might be paid less.

José continued a conversation with himself. "Look, I don't drink. I don't smoke. I don't cheat on my woman. I go to mass whenever I can get to town. I don't say ugly words. I don't bother anyone." He ticked off his virtues on his fingers. "And it's all because of my good soul. I trust in God in the sky, and I know someday he'll look down and see what a good man I am and . . ."

Ana quickly thrust the money into the man's hand. José feigned surprise. Lifting his battered hat and looking skyward again he intoned, "May the good Lord bless you my patroness, as well as all the saints." Then bowing awkwardly, José clamped on his hat, retrieved the rag cushion and the water can, and tripped out the door backwards.

She had almost invited him to sit down for some coffee and fruit. But then she recalled how plantation residents are notorious gossips, especially when a woman's husband had gone to the city. But this American, trained by a college journalism degree to uncover the story that every individual has, couldn't resist the chance to talk to the funny little water bearer. If she had been in the States, she would surely have interviewed him for a feature article.

Back in the 1950s someone interviewed my mother for a feature story in the *Topeka Capital-Journal*. The clipping from the now faded story includes a photo of a beautiful woman in a dark skirt and sleeveless white blouse. She stands beside a dump truck with a sign that reads, "Garrett Trucking." The story details how Peggy Anne Garrett had taken over her husband's agricultural lime business when he died in an accident.

After my dad died, my non-traditional mother always caused male heads to turn whenever she stepped out of a dump truck bringing lime or gravel to a construction site. The one featured in the article was Forbes Air Base, where she was helping build a runway. She also hauled aggregate rock for the Kansas Turnpike construction.

I'm not sure if Mother's early interview had anything to do with my decision to go into journalism. That probably had more to do with writing one of those "What I Did Last Summer" themes in grade school. When I embellished my third-grade writing with a few falsehoods that made it the adventure I craved, my classmates gave me so many affirmations that the experience elicited an unconscious drive to do more of that writing stuff.

A craving for praise. To hear the words, "Good job." That's what drove me through elementary school. But praise for my writing skill was not the only trait to carry me into adulthood. A more negative yearning finished the job and plagued me well into maturity.

Hunger was my driving force. Actual, physical hunger—for food, for affection, for family, for a stable home.

I didn't realize it at the time I became a Peace Corps volunteer, but the people I worked with in Brazil shared the physical hunger I endured as a child. However, their hunger carried the toll of malnutrition. Even death.

The plantation was bathed in humidity as José slipped down the hill. Should he buy some biscuits with the money Dona Ana had given him and surprise Joséfa, or use the two cruzeiros against his debt at the company store? A difficult decision, but he had all day to ponder it.

After completing his "woman's work," José fed Dona Ione's chickens and swept the cobblestone driveway, then the immense tiled veranda with its crowding of potted ferns and canvas chairs. From there he moved to the back of the *casa grande*. Here there were no decorations, nothing to break the bare utility of the maid's quarters but a few mangy canaries chirping in their bamboo cages. After washing lunch dishes, Severina was there setting out Dona Ione's pots and stainless-steel serving pieces to dry on the low wall that surrounded the back of the house.

"Aren't you going home for lunch, 'Ze Paulo?"

He shook his head sadly. If Dona Ione were here, he would eat meat, rice, and beans. But she was in Recife, and he would go hungry. Besides, why walk all the way home when there was only manioc paste and water? Better to leave that for the children.

The sun and intense humidity caused José's empty stomach to rumble as he watered the lawn—a task Marco insisted on, even in the rainy season. It was Hawaiian grass and dense as carpet. Marco had brought the seeds from Recife a year ago and under his watchful eye it grew to cover the quarter-acre lawn like a velvet blanket. It now looked good enough to eat, and José was tempted to experiment. But at that moment a chicken came pecking along, searching for bugs.

Those damn chickens were a curse to his service, he thought, then quickly made the sign of the cross to erase the bad word he'd just uttered internally. He chased the well-fed beast with the water hose, imagining it swimming in a delicious blood sauce—*Chicken Cabidela*. How long was it since he'd eaten that dish? The Feast of St. John two years ago. Maybe old Teresa, his neighbor, would fix it again this year. Only a month away. That thought sustained him until he was distracted by sounds coming from the stable.

"*Car-val-ho* (horse)! Get the hell out of the way, you beast of smallpox!" Carlos da Silva slapped the rump of one of Marco's fat stallions, but the animal ignored him and calmly continued eating its special ration of sugar cane leaves and grass. Carlos left the stable, slamming the iron door behind him. Being known as a *vaqueiro* (cowboy) was one thing, but shoveling horse manure and playing nursemaid to spoiled horses was not exactly in keeping with the image Carlos had of himself. From under the perpetual leather hat that had earned him the nickname *Chapeau*, or hat, peered black, resentful eyes. He turned in the direction of the Zebu steer chewing grass in front of the stable. He hated all of Marco's livestock, including the 50 well-muscled mules that carried sugar cane from the fields to the trucks for loading, the 100 head of hump-shouldered cattle that served no apparent purpose other than to make work for Carlos, and the three stallions that Marco allowed no one to ride. Sometimes, when the boss wasn't on the plantation, Carlos rode all the horses bareback to the pond for their daily baths. He watched them wolf down their ration and spat into the clay soil. *I should eat so good,* he thought. As he went back to the stable for more feed, Marco's Jeep rounded the corner of the corral and nearly ran over the stable hand.

Way before the days of food stamps, someone left a Thanksgiving meal at the doorstep of our little Nashua house on wheels.

That meal in a large grocery sack included an entire dressed goose, potatoes, vegetables, rolls, and canned goods. It appeared magically at our trailer park in Tulsa, Oklahoma. This occurred in a postwar era that saw few single women going it alone and trying to raise two young children. But my mother was adept at going against cultural norms. She single-parented far away from the concerned but critical eyes of her parents and other relatives back in Kansas. They had already criticized her for the relationships she cultivated after my dad died. She must have been desperate to escape the dull confines of her parents' house so she married my dad at 17 and gave birth to me at age 18. Two years later she had my brother Jim. Two years after that she was a widow.

Maybe she couldn't be blamed for trying to rediscover her youth. Maybe she couldn't help feeling the impossibility of raising children on her own in the 1950s. She left her third child, a son named Noel, at the hospital so he could be adopted by another family with a father in the house. Then she loaded my brother and me and all our belongings into a pickup truck pulling a new mobile home and hauled ass south, away from prying eyes and condemning tongues. Also, it wasn't her fault she was raised by an unaffectionate, stubborn, second-generation German father and a schizophrenic, demanding mother. Who could blame her for taking us through a tornado in Winfield, Kansas and finally coming to rest in one of the first-ever mobile home parks in the country?

And of course, she was fleeing the sociopath she may or not have married. After Mother died, we could never find a marriage certificate in public records. When he was with us, the man attempted to be a stepparent by beating me half to death and threatening to cut both us toddlers into little pieces. I would have run like hell too.

Thus, Mother found herself stuck in a trailer court with two hungry, sad-eyed kids. She tried to feed us and herself by working as a waitress at the Tulsa Airport restaurant. She left us in another trailer in the park with a woman who must have been having an affair with a night-worker living nearby. That would explain why our babysitter left a six and a four-year-old alone for an hour or longer at a time. But thank God for that! It gave me time to raid her refrigerator and inhale all the food I could reach.

When Young Mother Hubbard came back to discover an empty fridge, I pointed the finger of blame at my little brother. Whereupon she spanked him. Now, in my devious little mind, this was only fair, because Mother loved my brother best. And that favoritism was probably her way of paying me back for being a colicky infant and the favorite of my dad. Usually, instead of lying and getting Jimmy into trouble, I bossed him around and tried to protect him from harm, a job I'd taken on myself right after our dad died. I became an old lady at the age of four and often acted as the adult in our fatherless home.

As my mother partied, drank a lot, had provocative photo shoots in a muskrat coat that hinted of nothing else underneath, I kept my brother away from some of her lost-youth activities. Mother joined Youth for Christ and brought home some of her new friends. Our front yard in Topeka became the site of impromptu music fests featuring young men with guitars singing churchy songs and groping the young women sitting on their laps. I stayed in the shadows, way past my bedtime, giving them all a scornful, adult eye. Then I picked up after them. When Mother and anyone who might have spent the night did not get up to fix our breakfast, I often tried to do that too.

I was probably never in danger of starving. So many of the people I would work with as a Peace Corps volunteer in Brazil knew actual starvation and a physical hunger that I could never identify with completely.

Persistent beeps of the Jeep's horn brought José running to open the gate to the driveway. Uh oh! Senhor Marco! Time to brace himself for lots of running and fetching. Thank God the boss wasn't on the *engenho* (sugar cane mill) every day.

The Jeep stopped in the garage and a mustached, white-hatted man crawled out clutching a briefcase. Another man wearing a pastel-colored, lightly-embroidered short-sleeved shirt with square vented tails, the "uniform" of Brazilian males in the tropics, got out of the passenger seat. Marco had brought a friend today.

"Oi, Ze Paulo! Como vai? Tudo bem?"

Flustered by Marco's unusual inquiry about his well-being, José snatched off his hat, bowed stiffly, and stuttered, "By the power and grace of God in the sky, everything is fine. Because God is good, and his power is great." By then, José was gazing at the sky with his hat clutched over his heart. Just what Marco had expected.

"You see?" he hooted, slapping his legs with a white Stetson.

Marco's companion smiled. "You'd think he was a Protestant."

José was a devout Catholic. His smile dimmed.

"What's more," continued Marco walking toward the house, "he doesn't drink *cachaça*, doesn't smoke, and doesn't cheat on his woman. Yet he calls himself Brazilian!"

They were still laughing as they arrived at the front porch of the *casa grande*.

"Severina!" Marco's shout brought a young maid from inside the house where she had been dusting furniture.

"Senhor?" Unlike his other employees, Severina refused to be intimidated by Marco's commands and saw no reason to be humble in his presence. She wasn't even afraid to look him in the eye and refused to keep her head lowered in subservience. Rich men did not make her quake inside like they did José Paulo.

"Bring *cafezinhos*, quickly!"

Without comment, Severina turned and disappeared from the doorway as the two men settled themselves into the chairs on the breezy veranda. Driving 30 kilometers over muddy roads full of ruts and puddles had taken its toll on Marco's friend, a city man, who was beginning to regret accepting his former school chum's invitation to spend a quiet day in the country.

The two men said nothing until Severina brought out a tray with two demitasse cups and tiny spoons, a sugar bowl, and two tall glasses of water. She stood by, waiting as they drank their coffee, studying the newcomer with unabashed curiosity.

"Severina, go unlock my office and send José after Manoel. I want to get the payroll figured out before dark today." Marco placed his cup on the tray. "And see what you can scrounge up for supper. Tomorrow I'll send Cicero to market in Carpina for meat and vegetables. We'll be spending the weekend here."

Turning to his friend, Marco rose. "Vamos. I want to show you my horses."

It was a little after 7 o'clock when José started for home. The tropical sun had descended hours ago, and the air was now damp and cool. He waded through the mud in the road and with each sucking sound of bare feet he heard the echo of Marco's voice.

"José, clean those bird cages. Do you want the poor things to die in their own filth?"

"José, polish my boots."

"José, burn the trash, for the love of God!"

Marco's demands were more frequent than usual, probably to impress his city friend.

Not even José's mother had ordered him around that way when he was growing up, bless her dearly-departed soul. But then José began to feel guilty about his disloyal thoughts. After all, the fetching and carrying was his job. He had been hired by Marco to do all these things. And it was so much easier than working in the cane fields.

If only I had a little more to eat, I'd have more strength to work and it wouldn't be so hard. He asked God to send him some meat. Meat was what a man needed.

He stopped at the *venda* to buy some biscuits. The small store was full tonight. It was pay day. But José wouldn't be paid. Neither would any of the men now drinking *cachaça* (an alcohol drink made from fermented sugar cane) and gossiping with fellow workers. They put their drinks on a tab, which never would be paid. The system had been designed so all these workers would remain indebted to their "patron." It kept them in line and less likely to listen to those college students and factory men who had come out here a few years ago drumming up support for a union. These men in the *venda* knew their place and did not intend to bite the hand that fed them. None of them had been schooled, going to work in the cane fields as soon as they were tall enough to carry a machete. There wasn't a school on the plantation now anyway. They had to go into town, about 17 kilometers away, to get to the nearest school or church. A few of the workers, and certainly their women, had never even been off the plantation. Those who had made a trip to town for items the plantation store didn't carry soon became disillusioned. The store owners in town were known for cheating illiterate cane cutters.

José elbowed his way to the bar through the shoulders of drinking cane cutters. "A kilo of *bolachas* and some kerosene, please." The store owner recognized José and frowned. "Don't forget, you're 50 *cruzeiros* in debt, José Paulo." He turned to weigh the hard biscuits and was surprised when his customer produced two wrinkled bills from his shirt pocket. Then he grinned knowingly, "A present from the Americana, eh?" The store owner's remark brought immediate speculations from a few men near enough to overhear the exchange.

"What about that Americana? Nice and fat. And how about her legs?"

José turned to them in disgust. "She has a husband, you know." He turned to wade back through the knot of dirty drinking men but greeted a few he knew on his way out the door.

As usual, Ligeiro was there showing a photo of his newest girlfriend. "Who would even want a fat, American married woman anyway? Look at my beauty!" he grinned, showing a set of perfect white false teeth, then fielded a flood of inquiries about his latest *noiva*, an *engenho* girl.

Leigero was Marco's "confidence man" and carried a philosophy of life that promised to make him old before his thirtieth birthday—even more so than the cane cutters. This philosophy included lots of *cachaça*, beer, wild horses, and as many women as possible. At 22 he boasted of being twice married and the favorite of prostitutes from the nearby village of Buenos Aires to the larger city of Carpina. He fancied himself a world traveler and would always tell his comrades, "I've been everywhere. I know Nazaré, Carpina, Limoeiro, Recife, Caruaru... The only place I don't know is São Paulo. But someday I'll go there."

Ligeiro was a local legend. They say he killed a few men—a rumor that sent women and children running for cover in the cane when he rode by on his mule. That really unsettled him. He preferred to imagine them falling at his feet in adoration.

Ligeiro's limited duties as a confidence man left plenty of time for entering rodeos, which is what he would prefer to being a bodyguard. To compensate, he often traveled to nearby *engenhos* to vaccinate calves—a lucrative venture. But he always spent his extra money as fast as he earned it. One time he traded a gold-plated rodeo trophy for a skinny, sickly mule and always thought he got the better deal.

When you wanted to find Ligeiro, you looked first at the *venda*, then under his favorite banana tree, the secluded place where he led his conquests. He could think of no better way to occupy his time. He was Marco's bodyguard, but Marco's body was so seldom seen on the *engenho*, there seemed to be no substantial threat to his life.

José liked Ligeiro. You couldn't help but be attracted by his friendly manner and good sense of humor. Just the same, José was almost sure God didn't approve of some of the man's actions. He never went to mass. Said it was only for women.

José decided to leave before Ligeiro could finish a joke about a prostitute. He stumbled along as fast as his stubby legs could carry him, but it was at least a twenty-minute walk home over rutted clay roads and swollen streams.

No moon tonight. That was good. He only saw her when there was a full moon. The woman wore a long white dress, and her skin was white as summer clouds. She often hid in the cane along the road watching as he passed by. He whispered her name, "Dona da Fome e Morte" (Mistress of Hunger and Death) and knew she would eventually come for him. But not tonight, thank God. He crossed himself and shivered as the wind rustled the cane leaves and turned them into a dark, tossing sea.

-2-

THE DEATH OF A CHILD
AND A YOUNG FATHER

They never warned us we might be burying children.

In fact, I don't recall the death of a child mentioned in any of the informal or formal Peace Corps educational and cultural sessions we attended except perhaps as a vague malnutrition statistic.

"*Venha aqui, Dona Ana.*"

Dona Teresa motioned me out of the corner of the mud hut where I stood rooted in fearful silence. Reluctantly, I approached the tiny coffin where the other women worked, glancing covertly at the child's mother. Maria Elena stood at the open window of the hut's tiny kitchen, her eyes focused on the sugar cane that formed a curtain a mere six feet from the house, her face expressionless.

On this day, even her goat and chickens roamed in silence outside, never crossing the threshold to wander aimlessly about looking for crumbs under the table. The house where they usually had free rein now bustled with the activity of strangers. Not even the infant cries they had recently become accustomed to broke the silence.

"Here," said Dona Teresa, handing me a stem of stephanotis blossoms. I looked down at the cherub face in its infant-sized pine box. Underneath the child and outside the blossoms now surrounding his head I glimpsed a lining of cheap white muslin. At least his little head rested on a pillow of white taffeta. And now he wore a stephanotis crown of glory.

I fought back the urge to vomit as the sweetly sickening odor of the flowers rose from the stem that was mine to put into the coffin. Gently forcing a stem under little Manoel's lifeless neck, I arranged

23

the spray of white flowers on the pillow as artfully as I could with my shaking fingers. I shifted my brain and queasy stomach into a less intense space.

So, this is how poor peasants embalm a body. I wonder if they do this for adults as well. When is the boy's father going to show up for the procession to the cemetery?

In answer to my silent question, João Manoel shuffled into his house, removed his hat and peered into the coffin. One last look at his first-born son. This normally boisterous man, the supervisor of a crew of cane cutters, quickly averted his eyes and looked at the floor, but not before I caught the reflection of a tear in his eye.

"*Vamos, por favor!*" He motioned to the cluster of women who were finishing up their work at the coffin to leave the hut. Dona Teresa carefully positioned the lid with its protruding nails over their matching holes and pounded the cover softly shut with her calloused fist. She beckoned to the four neighbor children who had suddenly appeared at the open door to come inside. Without being told, they each grasped a rope handle on the side of the pine box and looked at João Manoel for the signal to begin the procession.

João looked at his wife with a silent question in his eyes. Dona Teresa gave voice to his query, gently asking Maria Elena, "Are you ready?"

The child's mother broke away from her window reverie as if noticing the crowd inside her house for the first time. "No," she said firmly. "I am not going."

My mouth gaped open in shock at the announcement that this young mother was not going to accompany her child's body to its final resting place. No one else seemed the least bit surprised, although Dona Teresa tried to coax her into the five-kilometer trip to Oiteiro.

Galvanized into action, Maria Elena shook her head no and abruptly shut the window she had been looking out of most of the morning. As the four children lifted the coffin off of the small table where she and João Manoel ate their simple morning and evening meals, the woman of the house brushed a few stephanotis leaves onto the floor. She seized a straw broom out of a corner and began sweeping the leaves out the door, pushing us all out with them. Glancing at my still-open mouth and questioning eyebrows she explained, "To go to the cemetery would be a *faz mal* (taboo). It would be bad luck and might keep me from having another baby."

I was the last person to leave the hut that morning. Maria Elena shut the door firmly behind me, remaining inside in the darkness. No one on this sugar cane plantation shut their house up during the daytime. But maybe she wanted to finally let go and cry over the loss of her child. She had seemed so devoid of emotion. Or maybe she wanted to pray. But had she said goodbye when little Manoel had taken his last breath? Had she blamed God? Or had she just accepted such a huge loss as a given in this harsh country, with its alarming infant mortality rate and short overall life expectancy?

I worked hard at slipping into a welcome state of sleep in the first few weeks after we buried my father. I lay flat on my stomach, head buried in a pillow soggy from tears. To wear myself out, I bent my knees and flopped my feet down on the clammy sheets, first on the right, then the left. The rhythm of the flopping feet and the answering creak of the bedsprings at the end of each flop usually lulled me to sleep. Sometimes I had to do the foot flops so rapidly, and make the springs squeak so loudly, so that the sound would drown out the voices.

I always heard them at night, never able to make out any words, but the voices rasped with urgency. I wish someone could have explained those raspy voices were my dad and my guardian angel in conference, trying to figure out who to send to console me. It might have stopped the foot flops.

They buried him on my fourth birthday.

Just three days before his funeral I had been celebrating with an early party on our screened-in porch. I was later told that my Uncle Glenn and Aunt Opal were staying at our house following the wedding of a relative. Our large, extended family always took advantage of such occasions by aggregating celebrations. My cousins and aunts gave me presents and we all enjoyed birthday cake and ice cream, the kids sitting cross-legged on the concrete porch floor. My dad had said goodbye to all of us just before the party. My voice followed him anxiously out the screen door.

"Where are you going, Daddy? Can I go too?"

"Not this time, Twister." (I had been nicknamed for the famous weather pattern of our state, probably because I left destruction and chaos wherever I went.)

My father paused in the open door of his dump truck, standing on its running board. "I'm going to earn you some pennies," he called back, knowing I treasured those shiny things, then waved his hand in farewell and blew a kiss. It was the last time I ever saw him. It was probably also the last time I would be touched so deeply by death. Until the day I helped bury a child in Northeast Brazil.

As I trailed behind the small procession of mourners, more questions swirled inside my agitated brain like *pipoca*, the Portuguese word for popcorn.

Why hadn't I spotted a problem with little Manoel a few days ago when I first visited his house? In contrast to other infants on the plantation, I would have shown off the three-month-old as a poster child of good health. True, as a supervisor, his father was paid a little more than most of the other sugar cane workers. So maybe they enjoyed better nutrition than average. As I held him that day, quickly returning him to his mother when he peed on my dress, he exhibited no signs of marasmus or kwashiorkor, the diseases of malnutrition the Peace Corps had trained the women in our group to look for. Good, rosy skin color—even rolls of fat!

He was too young to have developed Schistosoma from bathing in the plantation's polluted streams. But was Maria Elena giving him powdered milk made with polluted water? Like most of the area mothers, she probably wasn't breast feeding, preferring the Nestle's milk that had been distributed irregularly by USAID's Food for

Peace program in this area. If she mixed it with polluted water, without boiling it, maybe some virus or bacteria had caused a respiratory illness that quickly took his life. Or, what if it was meningitis? That can cause a sudden death.

Did Brazilians have to worry about Sudden Infant Death Syndrome? There was no evidence of a crib. Most Brazilian babies slept in a hammock with one or both of their parents.

Tripping over a rut in the clay road brought me out of my inventory of possible causes of death. I continued to trail behind the rest of the procession. The last time I had been over this road was on one of the plantation mules. I had managed to find Carlos, the stable hand, in a good mood that day. He even helped me saddle the perky-eared beast without complaining. He grunted in surprise as I put my foot in the crude wooden stirrups and mounted the mule that was easily 17 hands high. Carlos raised his eyebrows in admiration as I took the reins from him and poked my white Keds into the mule's flanks and headed to Oiteiro.

I didn't have enough Brazilian vocabulary to let the stable hand know I grew up around horses and watched every television episode of *National Velvet*. As a five-year old, I dreamed in equestrian and proudly accepted the nickname of Annie Oakley, preferring it to Twister. A girl who could ride and saddle horses at age six surely deserved a more fitting term of endearment. Besides, by then I had my own toy six-shooter and a cowgirl outfit that helped me get through a tap-dancing recital at Boone Private School in Topeka.

On a Brazilian beast that was only a little faster than the old mare named Bullet that I owned as a youngster, I had soaked in the beautiful scenery on that first mule trip. Meeting a potential teacher for the plantation school I hoped to open, I learned she was already teaching a few children in the mornings, then adults at night in her home with the aid of a kerosene lantern. She did all this teaching without pay. I guess that wasn't much different than all the state teachers in nearby larger towns who had not been paid in months.

There is nothing pleasant about today's trip. Matter of fact, it's drudgery and tragedy. I hate walking this far. It's hot. I'm sweating.

The broadcloth material that had seemed perfect attire for the tropics when I made a pair of culottes and a short, side-slitted overdress before we left the States did not breathe. In fact, it had turned into a water tank for sweat.

My predominant thoughts heighten the drudgery and discomfort. Just six months into our assignment in Brazil and I am questioning everything. Why are we here? How can we ever hope to accomplish any good in this place when we have to battle three centuries of entrenched poverty and misery? We yanked ourselves away from the comforts and fun of a college campus and the novelty of a new marriage to land in this hot place, full of dangerous creepy-crawlies. We sleep on a scratchy straw mattress at night and long for a McDonald's hamburger and fries by day. We try to coax our stubborn Germanic tongues into the silky sounds of Portuguese and meet questioning stares and laughter at our often-clumsy attempts to communicate.

My husband and I began our Peace Corps assignments on one sugar cane plantation, stayed three months, and then had to relocate to this place situated 17 kilometers from the nearest paved road. From the contacts we have occasionally with Peace Corps staff and the bureaucrats at GERAN, the national land reform agency that administers our work, we hear hints the program we have trained for will soon fall on its face. The sugar cane plantation owners resent GERAN for trying to control any part of their land, even the few hectares that were to be set aside for vegetable garden projects. And today I am helping bury a child I saw three days ago as healthy and in no need of any assistance I have been trained for.

As we finally reach the cemetery and the sweaty, tired children lower Manoel's coffin into a new grave dug out of the stubborn clay, I let the tears escape. Tears for this child, for my ineptitude in being any help at all to his family or the rest of the people in this God-forsaken place. Tears of homesickness and self-pity. Tears, even, for my own father, deceased so many years ago. I had vowed long ago that nothing like this would get through the gates of my locked heart. I would not show any emotion, any weakness whatsoever. I was a strong, independent American woman. I was Annie Oakley, fighting bad guys and ready to do battle against the forces of hunger, malnutrition, poverty, and ignorance in a foreign land.

God, why am I here? Why did we think we were needed in this place? How could we have been so idealistic and naive? Why are we not back home with our friends, protesting the war and joining the "revolution" against the crumbling status quo and hypocrisies in our own country?

But as the tears dry in in the tropical sun, leaving white steaks of salt down my face, I know why we're here. And why there is no going back. At least not yet.

PART II:

CULTURAL CONDITIONING
AND
CURRENT EVENTS

-3-

PENCIL-NECKED GEEK MARRIES DYSFUNCTIONAL INTROVERT

Spring, 1970 - Campus of the University of Missouri.

A group of one female and three male college students walks along the sidewalks of Francis Quadrangle. Two of the males wear combat boots and Army-green fatigue jackets with stenciled peace symbols where a name badge should have been. Underneath the jackets they have on the blue chambray uniform shirts of American workers. All the members of the group wear wire rim, round glasses. Males and female all have shoulder-length hair, except the one guy who had given up on his wavy, kinky hair. Length would have only made his mop look like a mountain man had escaped onto a college campus. But he made up for that lack of conformity by assuming the role as the group's intellectual leader. His ingrained, authoritative presence and superior air qualified him as a mouthpiece. He had, after all, won an American Legion Oratorical Contest in high school.

This leader, the eldest in a family of 11 kids, would occasionally show his wild side. He worked part-time at Nowell's Grocery Store in the catering department, a job he qualified for by having grown up with relatives who catered wedding and anniversary receptions. Sometimes after store hours he'd perch on top of the stainless-steel countertops in the grocery store's kitchen and, at the request of his co-workers, do a monkey imitation that would have caused real primates to pick his hair for lice. Later he would do a similar performance in South America, but there he imitated a great condor, bugging out his eyes until they nearly popped out of the sockets, and flapping his arms the way he

34

imagined the majestic birds doing. But he usually had to be drunk to accomplish that.

Dan's famous imitation of a Great Condor became a party favorite.

As the college friends ascended the stone steps leading out of the quadrangle that spring day, they quietly discussed the protest they had just participated in. The war in Vietnam was its fuel and focus. In fact, it had been fomenting protests on campuses all over the country.

The local sit-in had grown especially volatile, with an attempted takeover of Jesse Hall, the university's administration building. One of the more ambitious protestors managed to unfurl a homemade peace sign on a sheet and hang it out of a window on the top floor of the building. Students stood cheering and chanting all around the quadrangle at the sight. They also sat on the windowsills of other campus buildings, dangling their legs and kicking their heels against the stone walls in rhythm to the chants. A protest organizer, also wearing the 1970s uniform, used a bullhorn to list an inventory of abuses by government and university leaders. He called for a revolution.

35

In a less parochial context, the banner headlines on newspapers in Missouri and all over the nation had been shouting about the Mai Lai massacre in Vietnam. Five hundred civilians had been murdered, many of them women and children. Students fumed with outrage and erupted with righteous indignation over what we perceived as the calculated deception going on behind the war our friends were dying in. Soon our indignation and sympathies turned to the civilian Vietnamese casualties.

I went along meekly with all of it, merely pretending to be a hippie flowerchild protester. Underneath a disguise of bell-bottoms and tie-dyed T-shirts, I was really just the insecure product of a Midwestern family.

As the oldest child in my family, I managed to absorb—by accident or osmosis—my mother's work ethic and her constant search for men to make her whole. But a lawsuit by my deceased father's estate against the quarry company driver who hit him head-on and killed him gave me an advantage that Mother did not have. It allowed me to go to journalism school at the University of Missouri.

Mizzou is where I learned to overcome some of the shyness and lack of confidence that plagued my youth. In fact, my university experiences opened my heart and my horizons, landed me a husband, a journalism degree, affirmation as a wordsmith, and a ticket to Brazil. Not all at once, of course. Those three-plus university years also proved painful, awkward, often embarrassing, but ultimately, life-altering. It would take signing up for Peace Corps service and living in Brazil to complete my journey into a semblance of maturity.

The world was going through some cataclysmic changes in the 1970s. My husband and I were just a blip on the swelling tide of liberalization in attitudes and social mores. The era defined us and put us on our own individual trajectories aimed at doing good and helping the world. Somewhat arrogantly, we saw what we were doing in the Peace Corps in stark contrast to what we thought was going on in Vietnam.

Our together story of getting married, then living and working in Brazil, had its roots in a weekend trip my sophomore year at

Mizzou to the little town of Hamilton, Missouri. I was going to meet my boyfriend's parents. Jerry's dad was a Baptist preacher. Jerry and I got to know each other on a blind date when the girl he was supposed to go out with asked me to go in her place. And even though the two of us had dated just a few months, I was already enjoying visions of a wedding in my own Baptist church back in Grandview, Missouri. That's what college women in the late 1960s did—aimed for the only goal we'd been taught by our mothers to shoot for. We thought we would finally be whole once we found our Prince Charming.

I'm not sure what happened to that vision, but after the trip to meet Jerry's folks, we drifted apart. We rode back to campus that weekend with his hometown friend, Dan. I can still picture Dan turning his lime green 1959 Ford Fairlane around to go back to his house at the edge of town. He had forgotten to grab a foil-covered coffee can full of molasses cookies his mother made. We stopped at the end of his driveway while his dad handed the can through the window. I recall his mother standing back and to the side with nine of his 10 younger brothers and sisters.

Something must have captivated my emotions at that sight. They all seemed so happy and normal. Mostly, they seemed close-knit, not like my dysfunctional family. I sensed there were probably few violent arguments in that two-and-a-half story white home. And there was certainly some good eating going on, judging from the moist cookie I tasted on the trip back to campus.

I dredged up the scene of the happy family cookie handoff at the first dormitory mixer the next fall when Dan approached and asked me to dance. From that day on, Dan and Anne were a couple. We ate meals together in the cafeteria that joined the separate men's and women's dorms. I gave him the mother treatment I had formerly inflicted on my brother by making him study his way out of scholastic probation due to a previous semester of partying. He served as social chairman of his housing unit—the third floor of the dorm that was referred to by an Indian mascot name, adopted from the imaginary tribe of Fugauwies. And the colorful, yet tasteless motto they adopted was: "Where the Fugauwie?"

From high school on, Dan had seen and described himself as a "pencil-necked geek." Like me, he walked through his youth in a surfeit of self-consciousness. He seldom dated, carried a slide ruler on his hip, thick-lensed glasses on his nose, and a huge intellect in his head. A year into our relationship, Dan had managed to pull his grades up, enrolled in journalism school, and quickly absorbed the intellectual rhetoric of the day—totally anti-war.

We were walking with his roommates on campus one day when he announced he was considering becoming a conscientious objector and leaving that summer for Canada.

I looked at him in utter shock, maybe even gasped in my normal fashion (which he soon came to criticize as my drama queen mode). But here we were, recently-engaged to be married, and he had just announced his plans to leave the country for some idealistic bullshit. Those plans evidently did not involve me. And this was the first I had heard of them. He had not consulted his parents, evidently knowing it would break his mother's heart and enrage his conservative Republican father.

What probably really pissed him off was that I had not totally bought into his philosophy. But the really bad thing was that my reaction embarrassed him in front of his friends. That scene nearly ended our relationship. I guess he thought that when a group of us sat around at an off-campus party, some of us smoking weed and all of us drinking spolioli or purple passion from a plastic trash can or straight out of a bathtub, that I had bought into all the revolutionary rhetoric. When I would join him and our friends at one of several sit-ins and peaceful campus protests, he figured I was all-in on not trusting Republicans, our government, or the baby-killers in Vietnam.

He must not have realized how totally self-conscious I was the night I pulled my 34-A bra out from underneath my tie-dye T-shirt and stuffed it into the cuff of my bell-bottoms. He didn't know how broken I was inside, how I just knew everyone was looking at me and waiting for me to make a mistake so they could expose me for a total fraud, a pretend-hippie, and a complete mental and emotional wreck.

Somehow, we pushed through that defining relationship moment. He didn't go to Canada. He didn't disappoint his parents or abandon his fiancé.

We got married two days after my 21st birthday in a Catholic church in Kansas City he'd been attending while working a summer job there. We had already been to Pre-Cana classes at the Newman Center on campus, a requirement to be married in a Catholic Church. I meekly abandoned my Baptist dogma and declared my intention to raise my children as Catholics. I had never been strongly attached to any philosophy other than defining myself as someone's other half. I felt the need to latch onto anyone who would consider having me for a wife. I did not want to travel the path trod by my mother. I was marrying a man who would never divorce me like she had been divorced or abandon me with children to raise on my own, like she had been abandoned. Catholics did not do that to their women.

PLAYING HOUSE IN A TRAILER
IN A COLLEGE TOWN

I began married life with Dan on shaky emotional ground, thanks to our mutual relationship inexperience. I soon funneled my energies into establishing a home and completing our last semester in journalism school. We lived in a mobile home, probably a Nashua about the same size as the house on wheels of my childhood. The rental sat at the edge of our college town, on the last of several rows of trailers, and overlooked a sewage lagoon with open country beyond. That location suited our joint needs for expansive green vistas instead of high-rise apartment or dormitory buildings on campus or in town. We were both basically country kids.

We set up housekeeping in that single-wide cramped space. I unpacked wedding Corning Ware, commandeered a rough wooden cable spool from somebody for a coffee table, and started playing house like I had as a child. While the trailer was mostly bearable for a starter home, we both avoided the horsehair, scratchy blue sofa that satisfied the "furnished" promise made in the rental ad. The floor was more comfortable.

Things on an intellectual and spiritual level were a bit better in those last days on campus. I had won the lottery in landing a mentor in journalism school—one Thomas Duffy, nightside editor at *The Columbia Missourian*, the daily newspaper that gave students real-life experience in reporting.

Males and females alike feared Duffy's bark and his scorn. The stereotypical, hard-drinking, crusty editor would roar at students for a mistake or omission, and embarrassingly loud enough to be heard over the newsroom's typewriters and ringing phones. Maybe his critical nature just seemed familiar to me, having grown up with a shouting, judgmental mother. Sure, he intimidated me. But I gained his favorable attention on my first semester in reporting the night he sent me and a male student to cover a flood. He sent us with a walkie-talkie so we could communicate our findings to the newsroom once we assessed the level of the rising flood waters in McBaine, Missouri.

It was dark-thirty when we got to the town to witness residents loading pickup trucks with furniture and personal items as the overflowing Missouri River lapped at the sides of the road. The guy who came with me started to give his account of the situation to a rewrite student over the walkie-talkie. He must have succumbed to stage fright because he began stuttering and mumbling. I had stood by silently, having deferred to him because he was a male, using the time to write a lead paragraph in my head. When he could not communicate, I grabbed the walkie talkie out of his shaking hands and started dictating the story just a few minutes before the presses downstairs at the *Missourian* were scheduled to roll. As I wrapped up the situation, I heard Tom Duffy in the background saying, "Good job, Anne!" I lived in the glow of that compliment for the rest of the semester.

In addition to sending out nightside student reporters for the daily paper that served as the J-School lab, Tom Duffy co-taught a feature writing class. I fell in love with writing in that class, and with the power of words to inform and entertain. A little book he wrote called *Let's Write a Feature*, served as the textbook. That dog-eared paperback still occupies a place of honor on my desk. I treasure the main lesson the professor and the book instilled in my core: Everyone has a story.

By the end of the semester, Duffy gave us topics for an in-depth feature series. I drew the topic of a potential state constitutional convention. I fumed and complained at such a dull, abstract subject, failing to see its importance. When I voiced those complaints, Duffy just looked at me sternly over the top of his glasses and told me to get busy, because that was one of the three best assignments he had given out. In the course of getting busy, I managed to land an in-person interview with the governor. The resulting three-part series ran with banner headlines and top-of-the-fold placement on the daily's opinion page.

As I neared the end of my last month in journalism school, Tom Duffy called me into his office.

"I've lined up a feature writing job for you at *The Fulton Sun*. The position is opening in a month."

His good news came a few days late. We had just been informed by the Peace Corps that our application to serve overseas had been approved.

-5-

GIVING UP FOREIGN CORRESPONDENT DREAMS

One day in the early part of September of 1970, Dan and I rode together to campus. Both of us had early classes at the J-school, then he would be working at KTGR Radio giving the noon newscast. He majored in broadcasting, and our last semester he had been hired as a part-timer by the local pop radio station that had a studio on the ground floor of the Tiger Hotel downtown.

I loved watching Dan do his news reporting job, ripping the AP wires off the teletype machine a few minutes before he was set to go on air, jiggling his knees in nervous anticipation, and finally booming out a deep-throated, "This is Dan Chadwick, KTGR, with your noon news."

The excitement and romance of journalism always sucked me in, maybe because it allowed me to experience emotion and drama vicariously. Like music or a good movie, reporting and deadlines and being in the middle of the news could call up sentiments I never allowed myself to express or feel, having repressed them in childhood.

Even before my freshman year in college, after working on and editing my high school newspaper and yearbook, I had romantic visions of becoming a foreign correspondent. But upon confronting a holy terror named Sarah at registration for journalism school the semester before my junior year, those foreign correspondent dreams quickly poofed away. She was the real deal. A foreign correspondent during World War II, Sarah had been hired at Mizzou to help students map out their course of study for the next two years. Maybe she was tasked with weeding out the weaklings. Her tagline to

44

everyone was, "Did you bring a pencil? If you don't have a writing tool, you will not make it as a journalist." I had not brought a pencil. I had a Bic pen, but that was not good enough. "You can't erase pen," she said with a scowl.

Dan did not get subjected to that treatment in the broadcast segment of his studies. His intellect and voice put him on a quicker trajectory to potential success. It began with the radio station gig.

I wasn't there the day his idiot colleagues set his script on fire during a live broadcast. It was probably some kind of initiation to see if he'd keep his cool. He did. But what worried him the entire span of our last semester in school was a number; specifically, his draft number. It was 145. And as the war in Vietnam continued to escalate, so did our worries.

But that was before that day in the car on the way to campus. The day I had a sudden revelation—right there in our 1964 Plymouth Fury, the old-man-car he had acquired from his late grandfather's estate.

I turned to Dan in the driver's seat and surprised even myself. "We're going to do something overseas that will help a lot of people."

The next words came almost as quickly and just as unscripted. "I think we are supposed to join the Peace Corps."

-6-

THE PEACE CORPS BECKONS

Dan and Anne's big adventure in a third world country began in the early spring of 1971. We felt relieved to be on our way to Brazil, although I was a bit disappointed we did not get my first country choice of Afghanistan (retroactive prayer of thanks here). Both of us were glad the Peace Corps had put a stop to the order by his local draft board for Dan to report for duty at Fort Leonard Wood. Service in the Peace Corps fulfilled two years of the mandatory draft requirement of six years of service and functioned officially as a "waiver."

As we sat on pins and needles to see if the Peace Corps would triumph over the draft board, we experienced all the pre-approval protocols and red tape the government had put in place to qualify us to serve as overseas "ambassadors" for the U.S. The FBI conducted background checks, scrutinized our high school and college transcripts, and interviewed friends and neighbors. We filled out endless paper forms and scheduled medical exams. All the shots came later—rabies, typhoid, diphtheria, and gamma globulin for hepatitis. Too bad they couldn't inoculate us against microscopic parasites and common old things like roundworm, scabies, dysentery, and amoeba. We would be affected by all of them.

By 1971, when we began our volunteer service, the Peace Corps had evolved into a fairly well-oiled organization that had managed to survive the first several hard years of Washington politics. Like most baby boomers, we were convinced that John Fitzgerald Kennedy, our late great hero and architect of the Camelot we wanted our country to become, had come up with the idea for

46

Peace Corps. In fact, Senator Hubert Humphrey had first used the term in introducing a bill to establish a youth corps. He campaigned for the concept in the primaries against Kennedy. It took an impromptu speech by Kennedy at the University of Michigan in the last few weeks of the 1959 campaign to get the ball rolling. A comment of Stanley Meisler's in *When the World Calls: The Inside Story of the Peace Corps and Its First Fifty Years* resonates deeply with most who served in that new organization: "Now, as the 1960s dawned, a new mood was stirring: a need to take an active part in life outside campus, a need to enlist in causes."

That described our sentiments as we joined the 10-year-old corps of starry-eyed idealists who wanted to memorialize our martyred President by following his inaugural admonition to ask ourselves what we could do for our country, not the other way around.

Men and women who would become congressional, business, and intellectual leaders in the U.S. had already blazed a trail for us as volunteers in Africa, India, and Latin America, serving as teachers, medical volunteers, and community developers.

When we landed in Campinas, São Paulo, Brazil in March of 1971, we were almost smug in our certainty that we were doing something more positive for our country than killing people in another Third World Country. We sincerely wanted to help erase the international stigma of the "ugly American" in Latin America. Ironically, we did not realize until much later that we were just a different type of soldier, in a different battle zone.

All of us—volunteers, American soldiers in Vietnam, and the common citizens of Latin America and other Third World nations—were mostly helpless pawns of the big boys. We didn't exactly join their exclusive power club, but we closed our eyes to how they were using us. At least I did.

At first, our primary concern was adjusting to a foreign culture—the language, the food, the customs—and soaking up as much knowledge as we could, as quickly as possible, so we could do our jobs out in the field once we finished our training.

We had both graduated from the University of Missouri in December and by early March we were walking across the tarmac at the Kansas City Municipal Airport (downtown on the Missouri River, and now called Charles B. Wheeler Airport), hand-in-hand, after saying tearful good-byes to Dan's parents. We would not see any of our friends or family for two years and faced so much uncertainty as we left the safety of the country for the risks and insecurity of an unknown foreign place. Both of us felt nervous and excited as we said our goodbyes, but knew it had to be better than me seeing Dan leave for Vietnam and maybe not coming back. It's a good thing we didn't know then that Brazil would present a danger to Dan almost as life-threatening as the jungles of Vietnam.

The couple in the snow in the winter of 1971,
just before leaving for Brazil.

-7-

OUR BRAZILIAN TRAINING HOME

Our first home-away-from-home during training was a white stucco *pensão*, the equivalent of today's Airbnb. We had a bedroom upstairs in the two-story private house that featured a tiled courtyard with a deep laundry sink and concrete scrub board. A few volunteer couples met in the dining room for breakfasts of French bread, cheese, and fresh fruit, lunches of beans flavored with meat, vegetables, and cilantro, and served over white rice, and light evening meals of yams, more bread and cheese. *Cafe au lait* came with the morning and evening meals and *cafezinhos* (strong black coffee served with lots of sugar in demitasse cups) and a formed fruit paste sufficed as sweet treats after the noon meal.

Our homes during training were mostly places to collapse into bed after intense language, cultural, and technical training.

Journal entry, March 15—Had language interviews and sessions with Peace Corps staff today. Training starts at 7:30 a.m. tomorrow. I really think Dan is going to pick things up so quickly. He may even study for a change. Can't wait to go shopping. The streets in Campinas are a tourist's paradise. But I wasn't too impressed by the market. It stinks and the meat has flies on it. But I'm a product of a spotless, sanitized environment, so my standards will have to be lowered. Had some Guaraná today. That's Brazil's national soft drink made from berries grown in the Amazon rain forest. I like it better than 7-Up.

Sunday, March 22—*All we've done today is nap, listen to the radio, and study Portuguese for a few minutes. I wish there was something I had to do! Did the laundry by hand yesterday. Might as well get used to doing it that way. A few times today I've thought about how far away from home we are. I don't really miss the U.S. that much yet, but there's nothing here that's familiar. All our friends are new. It just doesn't seem like home. Maybe it will in time.*

I wish we spoke better Portuguese. After getting lost the other night we're not as adventurous as most of the others. Four of them hitchhiked to São Paulo this weekend and didn't even take their passports.

First Peace Corps training center in Campinas, São Paulo.

Many Americans who haven't studied romance languages or Latin American culture are surprised to learn that not every country in South America speaks Spanish. Brazil was colonized originally by the Portuguese; thus, we would be learning to speak *Portugués*. That was lucky for me because we found it to be a cross between French and Spanish. I had a semester of French in junior high, two years of high school Spanish, and even some college Spanish. The roots of many of the words we were learning were Latin and common to all the romance languages. I felt on pretty solid ground with the rhythms of Portuguese and even with the twist of nasal tones that seemed borrowed from French. Dan had taken German in high school but proved a quick learner. In fact, both of us would eventually earn top scores on the Foreign Service Institute language exams at the end of our Peace Corps tours. At that time, we even contemplated working for the State Department and continuing our foreign service but decided that being back home near family was more important.

The group of volunteers we trained with ran the gamut, from an Iowa couple in their 60s, to kids like us just out of college. Married couples were just starting to serve together in the Peace Corps. Besides the Iowa couple, we quickly got to know Rod and Dorothy from Ann Arbor, Michigan, and Russ and Sharon from Salt Lake City. Russ spoke nearly flawless Portuguese because he had previously served as a Mormon missionary in Brazil. His sweet wife opened our Midwestern eyes to a new realm of life that seemed as foreign to us as this country we were to work in.

It happened on Easter weekend. A small group of trainees loaded into a Volkswagen bus taxi for a harrowing overnight ride into Rio de Janeiro, navigating hairpin turns as we held on for dear life. That was our first introduction to offensive driving as performed by the seasoned taxi drivers of Brazil. I would soon learn how to gracefully get in the back seat of a two-door VW taxi without showing my underwear to the world while wearing the miniskirts that were the fashion in the 70s.

As I stepped onto the sands of Ipanema Beach that Easter

weekend, I realized the irony of having my first experience of a beach occur in South America instead of the Northern Hemisphere. Then I noticed Sharon wore what looked like long underwear under her swimsuit. My parochial Midwestern eyes suddenly opened to new insights about people from my own country with vastly different beliefs from mine—people who wear temple underwear as a sacred symbol of their commitment to a religious doctrine.

That was just the beginning of the cultural education we were to experience in the Peace Corps, an education that differed dramatically from the theoretical lessons we learned from textbooks and in the classrooms of Missouri University.

Our trainers were mostly Brazilians in their early 20s who spoke nearly-perfect English. Language training happened every day and was punctuated by in-class Portuguese conversation and enriched by assignments disguised as shopping excursions or cultural experiences. Our training staff worked hard to engage us, entertain us, and befriend us.

We had at least one American trainer, an employee of the Rand Corporation on loan to the Peace Corps Brazil staff. Howard was married to Tanya, a Brazilian, and they took us under their wings, mentoring us, inviting us to their apartment for dinner and telling us we had promise as successful volunteers.

Monday, March 23–What a day! Woke up at 2:30 this morning and got sick. Had diarrhea later and didn't go to language classes. Had to get a gamma globulin shot and two skin tests. Then Geraldo gave Dan and I and Dorothy and Rod a culture lesson.

There sure are a lot of don'ts for Americans in Brazil. Geraldo told us that we walk differently than Brazilians. They walk slowly and nonchalantly. The women hold their heads up high and walk gracefully. We walk quickly and purposefully, with our heads down, intent on getting to our destination. Brazilian women almost always cross their legs when they sit. It makes them look like sleek animals.

They have pedicures regularly, since they always wear sandals, and pride themselves on their beautiful nails. They take small, dainty steps and always look like they've just stepped out of a shower. You'd never catch them going anywhere in curlers or Bermuda shorts, like American women do in the States.

There are not too many no-nos for men, except certain sitting positions. Geraldo says in two years we'll be just like Brazilian women, and we'll really surprise our family and friends back home.

March 22, 1971–*We have Delano for language class now. Today we talked about the Brazilian system of dating and shocking cultural experiences we've had here. I mentioned the flies on the meat at the market.*

This afternoon Paulo explained all about seeds and everyone did a germination test. Mine is radishes. Later we went out to the agronomy institute to see their composting operation.

Russ went to São Paulo today and brought back an anniversary present for Sharon—a 400 cruzeiro guitar. Sharon tried to teach me the chords. I know C and G and I'm learning how to strum, sort of. It sure would be nice to have a guitar for those long nights we'll be experiencing in the Northeast.

After supper Dan and I went out for a pineapple sundae. Tomorrow night we're supposed to go see David Copperfield with Russ and Sharon. We finally had a letter from Dan's folks.

March 30–*We built a stinky compost pile today. Estrume (manure) soup is about the pukiest thing I've ever seen. Got rabies, polio, and bubonic plague shots today. The rabies shot is a little sore. After supper we went with Rod and Dorothy to a pasteleria (pastry shop) and did some*

window shopping.
March 31–*Our clock was a half hour slow this morning. We could hardly keep from going to sleep during language class. Maybe the vaccines are getting to us. And I feel so dirty!*

We built a canteiro (raised seed bed) in the back yard of the training center and planted radishes and carrots. It's a little hard to do all that stuff in a dress. I went shopping downtown with Sharon and Dorothy and bought a sack of apples, some cashews, a shopping bag, and a pair of swim trunks for Dan.

April 1–*We had an individual conference with Howard today. He says he likes what he sees in Dan and me and thinks we're going to adjust fine in the Northeast. Right now, we're having trouble adjusting to our typhoid shots. I had a temp of 100 before supper but feel fine now. Also have a bit of diarrhea but took three paregoric tablets. Tomorrow, we finish a panel on the government of Brazil. Today's panel was so dull.*

April 2–*Had a real good town meeting tonight. We're going to start having more activities at night like card parties and playing games and listening to Brazilian music. Marcia is going to teach us to sew and embroider.*

We had a discussion with Delano about Peace Corps and why they're in Brazil. It was a little depressing from our point of view. There's lots of untapped manpower here for a domestic Peace Corps. There's already been one program that's shown success. I'm just glad we had a chance to come to this country. Delano and others think there is a wave of nationalism appearing in Brazil. It's so different than the U.S. Everybody at home is so afraid and tired. We don't love our nation like Brazilians do.

Besides focusing on language and cultural dos and don'ts, our group's training fell under the Peace Corps' broad umbrella of community development. Our collective mission was for the men to establish community garden projects while the women worked to identify stages of malnutrition in children and teach hygiene, nutrition, and domestic arts to the women.

Anne talks to the pre-school students about hygiene.

In the wake of the military coups in Brazil in 1964 (supported by the United States, of course) a move was underway to build a middle class among agricultural workers, especially in Pernambuco, where we were to be stationed.

Our work sites were supposed to be on sugar cane plantations there, where generations of peasants had been working for a dollar a day under the old *patrão* system—in reality, virtual slavery. The "colonels" that owned the plantations provided housing for their workers and often paid them nothing, keeping them indebted for life through the company stores that furnished them with supplies and sugar cane rum. Those workers spent hours in the hot sun wielding a machete.

Because of the patrão system, Pernambuco had long been a hotbed of reform and revolutionary movements. The 1964 coups was at least in part a reaction to what the military and our own State Department deemed the advent of communism and leftist worker uprisings. The new government was trying desperately and despotically to silence and sideline dynamic and outspoken, left-leaning leaders like Catholic Archbishop Dom Helder Câmara. We were warned not to associate with known socialists like Camera (a warning we would one day ignore as we paid him a visit in Olinda, where he resided). We were also warned in training to never ever talk about communism, and never to display posters of Che Guevara or any other international revolutionary leader.

If we really wanted to shorten our stay in Brazil, all we had to do was get caught smoking marijuana. And that would not get us sent home. It would land us in one of the infamous Brazilian jails.

Prior to our arrival in Brazil, Peace Corps had negotiated a contract with an agrarian reform organization called GERAN (*Grupo Especial para a Racionalizacão Acucareira do Nordeste*, or Special Group for the Reform of the Sugar Industry).

At the same time it was keeping tight controls on average citizens, the Brazilian military government was making a show of conciliation with underpaid sugar cane workers in Northeast Brazil through GERAN. The goal was to take land not being used to produce sugar cane and convert it, or even give it, to cane workers to grow their own garden crops and ultimately sell their produce in urban areas. But we'd been warned that GERAN was already becoming a massive bureaucracy without much getting done. It certainly wasn't popular with the plantation owners, who resented any attempts to control the land that had been in their family for two centuries.

We were about to gain plenty of experience in the political and bureaucratic mess in Pernambuco. And some of the messes would be American-made, as federal sources of food aid were slashed or discontinued by Congress and no longer given to poor Brazilians. We would find ourselves moving twice, and our work stalled as it tried to move through thickets of contractual snags and outright opposition from the plantation owners. Yet we would begin our work with lots of optimism and enthusiasm.

8

TRAINING HOME MOVES
TO PERNAMBUCO

By May, our training site moved from Campinas, São Paulo to Recife, Pernambuco in Northeast Brazil, where GERAN, was located. It was also much closer to the sugar cane plantations where we'd be working. In Recife we got deeper into the technical aspects of small-scale farming for the men and nutrition for the women.

In the largest city in the state, the volunteers began immersing themselves in the culture and activities of a bustling metropolis. We eventually found the city market, with what looked like the same flies on the hanging meat carcasses that we saw in the south. But the market in Campinas did not feature piles of fresh caught fish, whale meat, and mountains of pineapple like the vendors in the Recife city market offered.

By day we continued our intensive technical training. At night we explored this new city and got acquainted with its dire poverty. This is the city rural agricultural workers streamed into from the semi-arid area of Northeast Brazil called the *sertão* when droughts and famine pushed them off the land. Here they built *favelas* or shanty towns on marginal, shifting land, sometimes even mud.

We could see the shacks leaning on each other under the bridges we traveled over by taxi to get to the old part of Recife from our training site in a slightly-upscale section of the city. Later, some of the volunteers, including Dan and me, read a slim little book in Portuguese called *Homens e Caranguejos* (Men and Crabs) by Josué de Castro that detailed the life cycle of these slum dwellers. The nauseating symbiosis depicted in the book began with the slum dwellers defecating out the back doors of their huts and into the canals their stilt homes perched on. The human feces furnished food for the saltwater marine life in the polluted canals. The slum dwellers fished in the same water they pooped in, then fed the crawfish and crabs to their families, all of them essentially eating their own feces again. Predictably, disease and death cast a shadow over that mini culture of destitute people. The canal area was so putrid that wealthier Brazilians and us foreigners had to pinch our noses to shut out the smell that permeated closed taxi windows as we crisscrossed the city. The smell was even worse during the rainy season.

The hotel in downtown Recife that served as a
temporary home between job sites.

Saturday, May 8–The old diary has been in the trunk for a while, and I've been too lazy to get it out. The weather in Recife tends to make one lazy. The rainy season has begun. Last night, after a trip to a small town where some of us will be stationed, we had to wade through water to get back into our pensão. We also had to scoot in to beat the monstrous cockroaches that wanted in too.

The restaurant we wished to go to was standing in water, so we went to the Doctor's Club, which is essentially a cafeteria for medical students and local physicians, and had Shrimp Americana. Dan had lobster.

Tom Brandt was with us tonight and made an interesting comment, "You think training is the most important thing until you get on your site."

Tuesday, May 11–Dan woke up at 5:30 yesterday and threw up. I had diarrhea, so we both stayed in bed. We did go to afternoon class though. The girls later went to the American consulate to view some Walt Disney health films we might use in the field. After supper neither of us felt good so we skipped a session with some professional cantadores (singing storytellers). Delano, one of our favorite trainers, was angry with us for that.

Tonight, we went out for ice cream. I had a hot fudge sundae and a coke. It would have been much more enjoyable if I hadn't had to rush home to go to the bathroom. Damn these amoebas! I've got to see Dr. Chamberlin (our local Peace Corps doctor) and get an authorization for a stool specimen or something.

Well, my hair is still wet but I'm too sleepy to let the fan dry it anymore. Maybe I'll soon get the hang of the toca, a technique that the women here use to give their hair body and let it dry naturally. It requires wrapping long hair in a circle around the head and pinning it in place, then covering it with a colorful scarf. So much better than bristly brush rollers or the empty soup cans I used in the States with this long hair of mine.

Part of our Peace Corps training focused on medical terms, medications, and a long list of things not to ingest. We knew, going into this country, that our access to the superior medical care facilities and treatments we enjoyed in the U.S. would be severely limited. That's why they gave us so many vaccinations. That's why we were given paregoric tablets as an essential part of our survival kits, even though we risked becoming addicted if we took too many. I believe it contains a bit of opium or something.

Almost all of us contracted some kind of parasite or bacteria that caused painful stomach cramps and diarrhea and vomiting. It was in the water, in the food, and on surfaces contaminated by flies and rats. It might even have been in the air. But it wasn't in Brazilian beer. And many of us took advantage of that, forgoing the carbonated mineral water we were told to drink instead of tap water. We weren't even supposed to drink water from the large clay water filters with a dispensing spout that were household necessities in even the poorest of homes.

Fecal contamination was a reality for the volunteers almost as much as for every poor or rich Brazilian. The lack of adequate sewage treatment facilities in most areas of the country was never considered a problem by the majority of city dwellers. Yes, there were sewer lines, but most of them opened into the canals and then drained into the ocean, unless they were interrupted by an obstacle along the way. And nearly every decent bathroom in the city—in private residences and public hotels and restaurants—featured a bidet. You were supposed to squat over those porcelain things, turn on the waterspout and clean yourself with a stream of polluted water. Brazilians did. But they also had waste cans next to the toilets and that's where one was supposed to discard the rough, crepe-paper toilet tissue when you finished doing your business. Thus, most bathrooms had built-in un-air fresheners. And you were never, ever supposed to flush the paper down the stool.

The bathrooms that featured bidets and sit-down thrones were far superior to the public bathrooms in service stations and bus stations. We quickly learned to travel with our own stash of toilet paper. Often we encountered toilets that had only a hole in the ground, covered partially by concrete footpads on both sides. Squatting and dropping drawers in a public restroom was not a favorite activity for any of us. And it took us a long time to get used to the public servants who stood guard in those places, trying to keep them clean, and handing out toilet paper in hopes of a donation from travelers in need of relief.

Our trainers never told us about this aspect of daily life. We had to discover that on our own. But they did warn us to never ever get a shot from a local pharmacy. The needles the pharmacist used were dirty and the pharmacies allegedly peddled illegal medications.

But there was a time when one of those risky shots from a so-called shady pharmacist saved Dan's life and opened our eyes to the risks we had assumed by joining the Peace Corps

Anne Spry

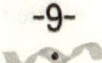

9

THE DAY DAN ALMOST DIED

We were nearing the end of our training and would soon be placed on sugar cane plantations throughout the state. Normally the men and women split into different training activities each day. I can't recall what the women were doing that day, but the men were out at the agronomy institute in Recife working with common garden pesticides they might be using in their garden projects. Who knows whether the guys were told to wash their hands after their Friday afternoon training session? Dan probably didn't wash his. At least that's what we finally pinpointed as the culprit in the sickness he endured within 24 hours of handling the chemicals.

At 2 a.m. Dan woke me up as he got out of bed in the *pensão* we stayed in. He soon came back and admitted he had vomited. Just as quickly as he settled back into bed, he bolted out again, running to the bathroom. By morning he was sitting in the shower, a totally weak wreck from hours of vomiting and projectile diarrhea. I could see the color had drained from his face and his eyes were glazed over.

Panic-stricken, I tried to give him paregoric tablets, but he couldn't even keep a sip of water down. Shaking from fright, my mind racing with morbid possibilities of seeking medical treatment in Brazil, I told Dan I would be back with the Peace Corps doctor.

I hailed a taxi on the main avenue a few blocks from our *pensão* and gave the driver directions to the Peace Corps office. Faith, the secretary, was the only staff member there that Saturday. When I explained in a rush what Dan was going through, she said the Peace Corps car was not at the office and she did not want me to use her car. Judy, a volunteer who was the only other person at the office that day, went with me to get another taxi to go to the address of the Peace Corps doctor. There we learned he was out of town for a week in the state of Paraíba.

Thank God we hadn't dismissed the taxi. We gave our driver the address for the Brazilian doctor on call for us, Dr. Carvalho. He wasn't home either and didn't even have a phone. His wife took us to a neighbor's house to try to call him on their phone. The neighbors were remodeling their house and workers had applied a varnish on the floor that made us feel like we'd been tear gassed. Besides, the phone wouldn't work. We went to yet another neighbor's house.

We became totally distraught upon learning the phone line to the place where the doctor went was out of order.

Back at the *pensão*, Dan's condition had grown even more dire. When I got back to check on him, he had just had another accident and wanted to shower, but the water was shut off, which was not unusual in this city with irregular public services.

Okay, now I was seriously distressed. In my halting, breathless Portuguese, I told the owner of the *pensão* I was afraid my husband was going to die right there in her bathroom. She looked at me in alarm and immediately called the pharmacist at the corner drugstore. Soon a woman in a white lab coat appeared in our room and gave Dan a shot, something called Plasil, designed to keep his insides from constant spasms. I eyed the needle suspiciously as she administered the injection, but realized a dirty needle was the least of Dan's problems. She left other medications and soon my husband was sleeping soundly. In fact, he slept well into Sunday afternoon.

That was the longest day in my life, and his too, I'm sure. My journal entry that weekend noted that he had lost 15 pounds since we got to Brazil, most of it in the previous 24 hours. I don't know how Dan felt, but I felt totally isolated, fearful, and afraid we had made a big mistake committing to two years in a country where health, and even survival, was nothing to take for granted.

But we had little time to dwell on our own vulnerabilities. Our brush with dehydration and death was nothing compared to what the poor Brazilians we would be working with faced every single day.

Journal Entry, Friday, May 25-Our technical training is over now. One day we went to a rehydration hospital and saw some pretty grim realities: babies so dehydrated they looked dead, with IV needles sticking out of their heads. A few days ago, we went to a school in a poor bairro to give a health lesson. Afterwards the kids all kissed us and asked for our autographs.

We spent three days in the field on Marti and Tom's site learning more about harsh realities.

We're going to the American consulate tomorrow, supposedly to find out about more things not to do. Joselda, one of the female trainers, advised us today never to tell anyone here that we're writing for a newspaper in the states, or it'll cause all kinds of problems. I certainly have been shirking my duty in that area.

Before leaving for our Peace Corps tour, I had met the editor of Dan's hometown newspaper and offered to become a "foreign correspondent," thus fulfilling my career aspirations. He quickly accepted and I did manage to mail several stories. Little did I know I would eventually become the editor and later the owner/publisher of that same newspaper.

PART III:

A HOME IN A HUT

-10-

OUR FIRST BRAZILIAN HOME

June 21, 1971, was moving day for us. By the time we finished training, everyone had been assigned to their sites on area sugar cane plantations. We were to live on Engenho Limão. Our house would be close to a paved road where we could flag down the bus to Recife just about any time during the day.

By that time in our lives in Brazil we had become adept at using the country's public transportation system. We took buses everywhere. In contrast to other countries in South America, Brazilians did not paint and decorate their buses in wild colors or hang good luck amulets from the sides and the rear-view mirrors. The country's truck drivers practiced those quaint customs.

The buses were actually not much different than American Greyhound buses, at least on the exterior. Inside the buses was a different story. Each one featured a chrome luggage rack along both sides and above the seats. Those racks were not filled with suitcases. Instead, you might see a few live chickens with their heads hanging over the side looking down at the passengers, immobilized by having their feet tied together. Or you'd see a basket full of produce or a sheet full of clean laundry tied up in a large ball. The racks also served as handrails for the riders who had to stand, sometimes for more than an hour. The vehicles did have a passenger load limit, but it was ignored in favor of more ticket sales. We quickly learned how to balance while standing in the aisles and traveling over bumpy asphalt, and how to brace for the sudden stops at every small town or wide space in the road on the way to the larger cities.

To stop a bus, all you had to do was flag it down like you

71

flagged down a taxi. It helped if you could whistle loudly, especially if the bus seemed to be passing you by. Thank God for wide shoulders along the pavement that allowed room for the buses to pull over out of the line of traffic. And thank God for reliable, mostly on-time bus service.

A few months into our volunteer service, we got acquainted with the *leito* or sleeper bus system in the country. What a wonderful way to travel long distances around the country! These buses featured fully reclining seats, pillows, and blankets and a "stewardess" to bring you soft drinks and hot wakeup towels in the morning.

Getting around in Brazil was really not a challenge, thanks to the bus system, the Volkswagen taxi fleets powered by alcohol, and the larger *comun* or commuter taxis that held up to six passengers and looked like the forerunner of today's SUV. When desperate to go somewhere, we even rode in the back of empty sugar cane trucks.

When we landed at our first Brazilian home, transportation was not a major concern. That plantation was also just a few kilometers from the town of Riberão, which we had visited frequently during training. Located about an hour outside of Recife, the town was a trade center for the many sugar cane plantations in the area. Several other volunteers were our "neighbors" on nearby plantations.

That June day we moved our clothing and a few other belongings into the row house situated close to the *casa grande* of Engheno Limão. Ours was the middle house and we had barely moved in before children and curious neighbors began peering in the open window and watching our every move.

We went to work immediately. And almost immediately we confronted bureaucratic problems and delays in doing that work. Another volunteer had been at the location before us and had managed to start a garden and work with local women to distribute milk and other commodities from USAID, but supplies were rumored to be drying up.

To complicate the situation, we knew right away this would only be a temporary home. Our final assignment and living quarters would be several kilometers from this one. In the meantime, we tried to settle into some semblance of a routine in a country that did not favor innovations or changes to its traditional social structure or economy. And at Limão, the departure of our predecessor had already caused some disappointments.

Our first job site on Engenho Limão.

Monday, June 21, 1971–Moving Day. Got moved into our site and cleaned everything up. It doesn't look bad. Stove works. We went thirsty for a while. The water out back is awful, so we boiled a lot of it. We got ready to have tea and coffee and I had forgotten to buy sugar. We had dehydrated pea soup and peanut butter sandwiches for supper. There were lots of people gathered around our door looking in, begging, and asking questions.

Tuesday, June 22–*Dan said he didn't need a blanket to sleep but he got under mine early this morning. It's pretty chilly here compared to Recife. We got up about 8:00, had tea and some old crackers from the barracão (company store) then got set to go to Riberão for groceries but some kids were working in the garden, so we stayed. The galpão (garden shed) is all cleaned up and the kids made a few canteiros (raised garden beds). The kids were mostly from one family. Maria seems to be the ringleader. She owns rabbits.*

After lunch we went into town. Dan got some wood for a rabbit cage and some shelving, and we bought vegetables, fruit, another blanket, eggs, a kilo of meat, and some bread.

Wednesday, June 23–*Today was the day to weigh children but I didn't know where the scale was.*

Friday, June 25– *We are not going to have any more oil and sugar from the USAID milk program. Also, it's not possible anymore to pay Dona Maria Teresa, the local woman who had always prepared the milk and weighed the children. We talked about the school lunch program and GERAN is not going to pay for it. It needs to be paid by the mayor or the community. The milk, however, was distributed today.*

Sunday, June 27–*We went to market at 10. There wasn't a good selection of vegetables. I think we're going to have a good opportunity with the garden at Limão.*

Monday, June 28– *Limão has 18 children in the first degree of malnutrition, 11 in the second, and eight in the third. When the mothers come to weigh their children, I will have to fill out new cards that will include the name of the father and the age at each weighing, so we can determine the degree of malnutrition.*

Tuesday, June 29–*I had intended to visit some families today but it's raining too much. I did finish filling out the information cards that GERAN furnished for families.*

Thursday, July 1–*Marcilio from the Peace Corps office in Recife and Thama (a Brazilian cooperative staffer) came here to talk to Dona Cecilia. Afterwards we went to see the house on a different plantation where we're going to live, but it looks like we won't be able to move until September due to the rains. The roads are too bad.*

July 2–*I waited all day for Daisy to come and talk to Sr. Reubem, the owner at Limão, about the school lunch program. She didn't show.*

I had to throw out almost a kilo of sugar today as it was infested with ants. Other bugs are ferocious today because of the rains. We haven't seen the sun for three days. Everything's soggy. Even the water filter has mildew on it.

I met the wife of the store owner today and watched her television for a bit.

Saturday, July 3–*Dan got the kids to clean a little in the garden. Glorious day. The sun's shining, but the flies are still tenacious. Did a huge laundry, washed a sheet, and even scrubbed our muddy tennis shoes. Got out the rubber gloves and went over the bathroom with Pine-Sol. We finally took a shower. The water wasn't turned off for a change. I baked an orange cake.*

-11-

CELEBRATING JULY 4
FAR FROM HOME

The large, close-knit family I married into knew how to celebrate the Fourth of July.

Dan's siblings had a side hustle every summer of operating a fireworks stand on the acreage they lived on. When the actual holiday finally arrived, after swarms of customers had shopped for mini explosives in the tent, the kids closed the colorful awning and got ready to party.

Carloads of their aunts, uncles, cousins, and family friends gathered in the yard for games of softball, followed by mountains of homemade food laid out on plywood sheets mounted on sawhorses. As dusk fell, the smallest kids abandoned igniting their smoky "snakes" and entire packets of Black Cat fireworks and gradually settled on blankets on the lawn with their parents or cousins sitting above them on lawn chairs. That's when my brother-in-law, Bob, put on a fireworks show with his excess inventory.

After the last aerial display faded from the black sky in trails of sparks, the family matriarchs opened canisters of homemade ice cream. We lined up to make choices between regular old vanilla, butter brickle, chocolate, or tropical sherbet. Then we had to choose between Texas sheet cakes, fruit pies, and brownies. After gorging, we all went home with a renewed sense of family connections but also to face a night of fitful sleep plagued by indigestion.

The fireworks stand became the launchpad for Dan's brother's entrepreneurial spirit, which he would later use to become a successful real estate agent. The fireworks sales also helped Dan out of a tight spot at the university one year when he came up short on tuition.

With that kind of family legacy, Dan and I were both dreading our favorite holiday so far from home, family, and friends. But we had a party of our own with volunteers stationed on a nearby plantation.

Once we got past a huge culture shock that first July 4th, we powered through other missed holidays that followed. We would spend a homesick Thanksgiving on the beach with other volunteers and a lonely Christmas eating canned Spam in our little mud hut while playing Christmas carols on a cassette tape player. But the thing that I remember most about that first July 4th in Brazil was the flies.

Susan and Dick were single volunteers stationed at Engenho Soledade. We met them that day for lunch at the Hotel Riberão, a popular gathering place for American volunteers. We ate at the hotel's outdoor cantina. By then we'd all been in Brazil long enough to land on a go-to, quick meal, discovering we couldn't go wrong with a sandwich called a *misto quente* (hot ham and cheese), topped off by the male volunteer's favorite beverage, a beer called Brahma Chopp. The Brazilian beer was originally made by a brewery founded in 1888, no doubt by the flood of German immigrants who settled in the temperate, southern part of Brazil. Not surprisingly, the Brazilian beer brand is now owned by Anheuser-Bush.

The volunteers had a joke about the beer. If a fly landed in someone's brew, it was customary to pull out the insect and wring it out over the mug, so as not to lose even a drop of the liquid. I guess it was that good. I never found out. I stuck to my *agua mineral* (mineral water) *sem gas* (without carbonation), or a frosty bottle of Coca-Cola (but never poured over ice made with polluted water).

As we all left the hotel that day, we headed to the plantation Dick and Susan worked on. Like us, they lived in a row house covered by whitewashed stucco. But their hut was directly across from the plantation owner's cattle pens.

We had bought cake, ice cream, and a bottle of gin for our little

Fourth of July *festinha*, so we stowed all that in their kerosene refrigerator and Susan and I set out to weigh babies and distribute some USAID powdered milk. Once that was done, we came back to their hut and Susan opened the window over the kitchen table. We got busy preparing a meal of hamburgers cooked on their kerosene stove, and made some good old American potato salad, coleslaw, and baked beans.

I don't think I had much of a stomach for that traditional July 4th meal. While our backs had been turned preparing food, the flies that plagued the Zebu cattle milling about in Dick and Susan's "front yard" had left the pen for the greener pastures of Susan's kitchen table. The red and white checkered oil cloth that had covered the table was blanketed entirely with a nightmarish, moving mass of black insects that ignored the fly paper strip dangling over it. I looked at Susan with horror, a question mark on my eyebrows, but she shrugged her shoulders. She and Dick were used to it. I'm just glad we were all young and healthy.

I may have opted to eat my holiday meal standing up outside the kitchen somewhere instead of sitting at the fly-covered table. The four of us finished off a bottle of gin that night and somehow managed to record an audio tape for the older Peace Corps couple from Iowa to send home to their kids. Despite the cultural shock of the flies, we had lots of fun and kept our minds too occupied to slide into homesickness and self-pity. We got back to our own row house at 11 p.m. By then we knew that our stay at Engenho Limao was not to last much longer. Certainly not the length of our two-year assignment. In the meantime, we had work to do.

Tuesday, July 6–We have a cat now. It's only a few days old and its mother died. We've been feeding it with an eyedropper, but it has to be forced to eat. It sleeps in the hammock with Dan's blanket. It will probably die when we go to Recife this weekend.

Dan ran films through the Peace Corps projector and spliced the broken pieces, something he learned to do in

TV broadcasting class. Meanwhile, everyone was at our door thinking we were showing them already.

Wednesday, July 7–*Milk distribution today. I went to Miriam's house to take some medicine and bring her kids to weigh and fell in the mud on the way. There are lots of slippery log bridges to walk across. A mother with a month-old baby says she doesn't have any milk and wants some from the program. I just don't know what to do. He could die if he gets diarrhea from a different kind of milk.*

Friday, July 9–*Our meeting with GERAN was called off but we went to Recife anyway, leaving the cat with Cecilia. We went shopping and I bought boots and sandals and other things we needed from Viana Leal, Recife's large department store. It even has an escalator! We also bought a gas refrigerator for $1,350 cruzeiros and had it tested. We were going to go home but were too tired. Instead, we stayed behind the Peace Corps office in hammocks strung from the posts of the pergola.*

Saturday, July 10–*I typed a story for the Hamilton paper on the Peace Corps typewriter and mailed it. Rod and Dorothy came in and we had hot dogs and banana splits at Lojas Brasileiras then went to Patio do São Pedro, a popular tourist spot in the old part of Recife. Later we went out for more grocery shopping and decided to stay another night in Recife.*

In all three of our houses in Brazil we tried to furnish and arrange them with as many of the conveniences of home as possible. We were a bit constrained by what we could afford on our monthly Peace Corps stipend. At the first home we managed to bring in a kerosene refrigerator and a plastic rocking chair. The latter had an iron frame shaped into a rocker and wrapped with hollow blue plastic cords. It turned out to be every bit as comfortable as any rocker/recliner in the States, except that sweating in the tropical climate while sitting in the rocker would cause your skin to stick to the chair and leave indentations on bare legs.

Brazilian hammocks, especially double sized ones,
are incredibly comfortable.

The refrigerator was an absolute necessity, since we became determined to fix meals that reminded us of home. We had a lot of trouble adapting to the Brazilian diet of beans and rice, although if we had, we wouldn't have needed a fridge.

Sunday, July 11–We finally got into Riberão on the bus and did feira (market) *quickly. I waited for Dan while he acted as an interpreter for some Americans who had an accident last night. The guy worked with SUDENE for the UN and his son is a 10th grade dropout with freaky hair. His father is a little freaky too. Brazilians said they were drunk when the accident happened. They asked for a bottle of sugar cane rum afterwards. The father thinks his diplomatic immunity is gonna protect him from any responsibility.*

July 12–Dan went to Recife to pick up our refrigerator and go to the bank. A man came by really mad about someone robbing his sweet potatoes in the garden and acted like it was my fault.

The cat cried almost all day. Dan got back from Recife about 5 o'clock. The refrigerator takes up quite a bit of space but it sure is good to have it. We had cheese hot dogs and soup for supper.

July 14–It seems like the days are stretching out endlessly. I went to visit Maria Teresa and didn't have to watch out for cow diarrhea because I had my new boots on. The cows here have lots of intestinal problems. Maria T. is really grippada (has a cold)–congested chest, rasping breath. I sent our Mentholatum to her with Rosinete. Ivonete came back wanting to borrow some oil.

I worked on milk records. Have 22 mothers to visit before next Thursday. I don't know what to do for a class that day. I'd like to start a new program. I studied a little Portuguese, did a little embroidery, but my eyes got tired. Dan went to the garden for an hour. I've been reading the rest of the day.

July 15–Marcilio, Susan, Dick, Miguel, and Estella came while we were eating lunch. They brought three letters from home.

My brother Jim is married, and Debbie is three months pregnant. Dan's dad wrote the funniest letter. Dan read the rest of the afternoon while I went to a sewing club meeting. We had spaghetti for supper and watched the cat run around.

July 16–Dan said I snored loudly last night. It must be because I'm getting a cold. We had biscuits for breakfast.

They didn't raise much but were delicious. We have enough for tomorrow too. We went to Riberão to meet with Dick and Susan about the milk program. It doesn't seem likely we'll get more milk after this supply runs out. Dick and Susan then came out for pizza and gin. We got into some hairy discussion, but I don't know what it was about because I was trying to make the pizza. We listened to a Peter, Paul and Mary tape, then they caught a 9:15 bus to Recife. Dan was not feeling good when we went to bed.

July 17–Dan got sick last night and still feels blah. I weeded the flower garden today with help from Cecelia and Horacina. I don't know what else I'll plant there. We do have a tomato plant we didn't know about. The cat is finally learning to lap her milk.

July 18–Went to feira and it was really good today. Bought a pineapple, six huge oranges, three bunches of bananas, 1 kilo tomatoes, green beans, potatoes, green peppers, onions, and margarine. Went to Mass but couldn't hear a thing for the loudspeaker in the plaza playing "Be My Baby." We met the priest after mass. He said he'd like to have me teach nutrition classes in his school. I wrote letters the rest of the day while Dan watched a futebol game—Pelé's last.

July 19–I mended Rosinete's dress tonight and Sr. Reuben came over. We gave him some gin, talked awhile, then he invited us up to the casa grande where we watched TV and ate supper. I borrowed a book from them. They're not so scary anymore.

July 24– Sr. Reuben took us to Riberão where we caught a commun (large communal taxi). We caught Rod and Dorothy in town and rode in the back of a sugar cane truck to Bonito, the engenho where they work. It's so beautiful and relaxing on that hill. I'd love to live in a spot like that. We had stroganoff for supper, then talked until real late. Oh, almost forgot! I took my first burro ride.

Recife, July 26–Both of us woke up sniffling and feeling out of sorts but we did have a great time with Rod and Dorothy on their site. We took a taxi to our favorite pastelaria and had chocolate eclairs and coke for breakfast, took some film in for processing, and went shopping for an anniversary present for Rod and Dorothy. It took us all morning and we still weren't satisfied. We got them a tablecloth and cloth napkins.

We grabbed a sandwich and headed for home. I had diarrhea so bad and didn't think I'd be able to make it without getting off the bus and going in the sugar cane fields, or else messing my pants. It was awful. I was so glad to get home and lie down. I took a cold pill and woke up dizzy, slopped a supper together and washed the dishes.

One of the most sanity-saving and essential items in our Brazilian household was our book "locker." The Peace Corps gave each volunteer or each couple a large cardboard box with the top and bottom inserted with cardboard shelves. Those shelves were stuffed full of paperback books of American bestsellers. Dan and I both read them all on the long, lonely nights spent on the sugar cane plantations. I'm not sure if the *Lord of the Rings* trilogy was included in the locker, but I became addicted to fantasy fiction in Brazil. Once we could read in Portuguese, we supplemented the library with Brazilian books. In the large wooden sea crate that we shipped home at the end of our service, I packed the complete works of famous Brazilian author Jorge Amado. Still, we gravitated to American works and took every chance possible to go to movie theaters to watch American films with Portuguese subtitles. We were often the only people in the theater to laugh at certain places in those films, because we were watching it in our native language and catching all the funny lines before Brazilians had a chance to read the Portuguese.

July 27–Both of us are a little miserable today, coughing and sniffling. I finished To Kill a Mockingbird. Fantastic book! Dona Zumira came to talk to us. I told her I'd be interested to teach nutrition classes. Dan was a little inarticulate about his plans for the garden, mostly because of his cold. I can't wait to get in the school and start teaching. We found a leak in our stove valve. The tank is almost empty.

The English class we taught in Riberão was lots of fun and I wasn't the least bit nervous. Doubt if they learned very much but I wasn't very organized. I will be next time.

July 29–Reuben's brother, Antonio (the rich one who owns the hotels), took us to Riberão for a meeting at the Institute this morning. It was about Kwashiorkor, a type of malnutrition, and several GERAN people were there. Sharon came in on her new horse. Russ is raising goats already. Miguel had an argument with Marcilio about his site. I guess he wants to come to Limão. Marcilio came over here later with Dick and Sue, all of them really beat. It looks like we move out of here next week and go to Recife for some in-service training and to laze around until we can move out to our new site. Dan will be in Carpina a week for rabbit training and there's a Peace Corps art cooperative I can look into. Other times I'll be going around in GERAN with Susan and going to the beach.

July 31–Dan went to get some horses this morning, but Reuben's grandkids and nieces and nephews had all the saddles. We stayed in and read all day. Got so sick of staying inside, just went out and sat on the porch. Got the ball out and Dan and Rosinette played with it. It fell on the orange tree and got a hole in it, so he gave it to the kids. If we didn't know we had to leave next week, we probably wouldn't be so bored.

August 1*–Got up a little late and gulped down our tea just in time to catch a rural* (an eight-passenger, boxy-shaped commercial taxi) *into feira. Then we went to the hotel to wait for Steve and Stella, who never showed up. There were two fortune tellers at the hotel swindling people out of five cruzeiros. Dan had a beer with the Oberhausers, then we left at noon. We told the kids at Limão we were leaving this evening. They acted a little upset and disappointed. Rosinete was downright mad.*

12

AN INTERIM HOME
IN A RECIFE HOTEL

One of the first things we observed as full-fledged volunteers was the tendency of all us Americans to gravitate to the familiar things of our own culture. There was a danger in that. We could have stuck with our own and never assimilated into Brazilian culture, never come to know Brazilians or make lasting friendships. The time Dan and I spent between the first and second site assignments could make or break us, give us the impetus to keep forging ahead to try to fulfill our roles as "ambassadors," or send us sniveling and complaining back to the U.S.

Instead, our hotel living in Recife gave us a nice break from the obstacles and bureaucracy we'd already witnessed in the few short months we lived on the first sugar cane plantation. We reveled in our American friends as they came into Recife for supplies and in the activities we all enjoyed. We purposely sought out everything that reminded us of our lives back home—from drinking cocktails at the Doctor's Club to discovering a restaurant that served strawberries grown in southern Brazil.

By the time we moved to our second sugar cane plantation, we had passed the milestones of our first July 4th in Brazil, my first birthday, and our wedding anniversary. Yes, we were homesick, but still full of do-good optimism and faith.

We never once considered doing anything but meekly going where our superiors sent us. But our eyes began to open to the fact that our Brazilian program sponsors might become even more resistant to working with Americans. And we also began to realize that change and progress in this part of Brazil would probably not happen as a result of anything we might attempt, despite all our do-good intentions.

August 11–Well, we're moved off Limão and are living in the Parque Hotel in Recife. Steve and Stella are at Limão now, taking care of our ailing kitten and fighting off the monstrous mosquitos. The way Stella acts, she doesn't like it much out there. The night we moved out we had to stay in the Riberão Hotel, where I got bit by a bedbug and caught the sheet on fire with a Citronella. What an exit!

We have found a restaurant in Recife that serves fresh strawberries with whipped cream, so we celebrated Rod and Dorothy's anniversary last weekend with the strawberries instead of cake. We also went to the beach, but the water was so cold Dorothy and I didn't get in.

We went to a meeting at the Peace Corps office on Monday. Yesterday we went through GERAN and talked to several different chiefs, including the #2 man, Chaves. He was especially receptive, but many GERAN people are really afraid and suspicious of volunteers. I hope we can do something to change that image.

We have checked into room 40 at the Parque Hotel, with its balcony view of a church and treetops and with a constant breeze coming in our window. We may learn to like it better here than in the campo (country).

At La Barca during lunch a man came up to our table and started scooping our leftover rice into a plastic sack. The waiter got really mad and made sure my purse was still there before he kicked the guy out. He stood at the door very indignantly saying he was dying of hunger.

August 30–Last week the female volunteers had a training session for literacy class professors. We got home at 9 o'clock Friday, my birthday, and found 11 letters in the mailbox. Dan came in shortly afterwards with some strawberries. On Saturday we celebrated our anniversary with Rod and Dorothy by going shopping, to the beach, out for drinks and dinner. We were going to play pinochle, but everyone fell asleep.

Rod and Dorothy went back to their site so Dan and I went to eat at La Barca again, then to see Beneath the Planet of the Apes. Rotten movie. We made up for it by getting daiquiris at the Doctor's Club. Today we checked out of the hotel after a breakfast of banana pancakes and tea and went to GERAN.

PART IV:

MAKING A HOME IN A HUT ON A SUGAR CANE PLANTATION

13

HOME ON ANOTHER SUGAR CANE PLANTATION IN THE MIDDLE OF NOWHERE

I wish I could see Tamataupe de Flores today. I tried to find it a few years ago using Google Maps but that was before the app became detailed and sophisticated.

Tamataupe de Flores' *casa grande* and stables and the old sugar mill had been built in the bottom of a deep bowl of red clay. That bowl always flooded every rainy season and would hold us as unwilling but ever humble foreign captives.

The day we arrived at our new foreign home, I do recall gazing in open-mouthed wonder at the green lushness, the tall, swaying palms that marked the creeks and waterways, the abandoned smokestack of the sugar mill, and an old Dutch church that perched on the ascent of the road leading to the next nearest settlement. All those things punctuated the plantation with memorable landmarks that soon became the familiar sights we sought out anxiously anytime we returned from forays out to civilization. It was beautiful, this place we called home for a time.

The memory of Tamataupe de Flores is cemented in my psyche. I can see the footprints we left in the cool mud near the pond during the rainy season as we walked between sleeping Zebu cattle to make the climb up the hill to our hut. I can smell the *estrume* the cattle left behind as it mixed with the clay and the remnants of their ration of sugar cane leaves. I can also smell the acrid but appealing smoke of burning sugar cane stubble and picture the line of fire rising up hillsides on a moonless night. And I can still hear the drums at midnight from a distant hut where a *Macumba* (voodoo) ritual was taking place. I can even imagine all these sights, sounds, and smells as if transported back in time to days when slaves from Africa cut the sugar cane on this plantation.

The three-room hut on Tamataupe de Flores.

In this Brazilian Garden of Eden, we finally made some progress in our do-good mission. We helped some individuals who needed it desperately. We grew as individuals and a couple. We checked off several things on our to-do lists. But we also got depressed, homesick, and fought with each other. We would become even more frustrated in effecting any kind of lasting change or progress in this beautiful, remote place.

My journal from those first days in our second Brazilian home reflects a large gap between August of 1971 and February of 1972. We moved in September, as I recall.

The first night we arrived, intending to stay in our freshly-painted hut with concrete floors (instead of the dirt floors found in other dwellings on the plantation), we slept at the *casa grande* instead. As we walked into our new home in excited anticipation, grateful for solid, clean floors and whitewashed walls with high ceilings, I stopped cold. In the kitchen I spotted an immense termite nest near the apex of the tile roof and inside the kitchen. No way was

I going to sleep in this place until that nest was gone!

The view of the casa grande and barns at Tamataupe.

During those months of no journaling, we had somehow managed to purchase a 1947 Willys Jeep. The Jeep was against Peace Corps rules. We were supposed to be living like the people we were working with, none of whom would ever be able to afford a vehicle. Peace Corps staff knew about the illegal vehicle and eventually we had to get rid of it. But it served us well while we had it. It helped us get out of the plantation and back to civilization occasionally, except during the rainy season. That Jeep also served as transport for some of the poor people on the plantation into the nearest town, Nazaré da Mata, to see the doctor.

The only other transportation out of the place was in the back of a sugar cane truck, while standing and holding onto the wooden truck slats as we bumped over rutted clay roads.

Those roads presented a huge challenge for the Jeep, especially after heavy rains. We often had to make a few running starts to climb the hilly roads and got stuck many times.

Our 1947 Willys Jeep.

Getting used to the perils of the rainy season was just one of many adjustments and learning experiences.

Tuesday, February 1, 1972–I can't figure out where my squeamish stomach went. Today I squeezed a boil and bandaged a bad cut. These people are going to start thinking I'm a nurse.

Supper is on the stove and I'm waiting for Dan to get back from Recife. He must've taken the 6 o'clock bus back. All I did today was embroider and find out some juicy gossip. Maria, the casa grande cook, is sleeping with Manoel, the storekeeper, and doesn't try to hide it. Apparently, Manoel's wife went to Recife to buy a revolver to shoot Maria, but no one thinks she has the courage to do it. Quem sâbe (who knows)?

Thursday, Feb. 3–*Dan left the key on in the jeep last night and it wouldn't start, even by popping the clutch. He went to buy construction materials for the water tank he's building for the garden project. Yesterday was more or less productive. I went riding on a mule in the morning to visit local families and talked to José Salviano about his medicine. Dan is going to see about that today. I also recruited a few girls for embroidery class.*

After supper Dan and I made a list of things we have to do in the next two weeks. We're going to try to have a meeting with the people about the garden. I need to clean house today in case we have a class here tomorrow.

Friday, Feb. 4–*We had class in the church instead of our hut. The old, whitewashed structure of adobe was built in the time of the Dutch occupation of Pernambuco in the late 1700s.*

In order to have the meeting there we first had to sweep out bat dung three inches deep and burn thousands of wasp nests. There were 13 girls, not counting the extras who came to watch. I started off a little stupidly, but everything turned out fine. They learned two stitches. They all concentrated so much on those little squares of material, it's pretty obvious they want to learn. When we were closing up the church, a man passing by came in to pray. It's a shame the church has been shut up so long. There should at least be some saints' statues. Wonder how a person goes about getting saints? Maybe the bishop has some lying around someplace.

Dan took José Salviano to Nazaré today and he was put in the hospital. Poor man. Manoel Dede said he used to be one of the strongest men around here. He's nothing but bones now.

Saturday, Feb. 5–I'm waiting to take a bath at the casa grande. The truck didn't go today to pick up class materials because some cane burned at a nearby plantation, and they needed it to help the owner. One or two may go tomorrow. That means I have to go to feira by myself or at least drive the Jeep all that way.

Among the first of our plantation neighbors to greet us were sisters Luisa and Zezinha (the latter nicknamed Nita). They were in their late teens, and both attractive young women with mostly-white skin. In Brazil, the lighter your skin, the better your chances were to lift yourself out of poverty or to marry well. Nita was already dating the plantation owner's young bodyguard, Ligeiro. Luisa was the younger sister and had not started dating yet when we first met her. Both the girls spent a lot of time in our house and were the first to take the embroidery and sewing classes that I began to teach.

Students in sewing classes at Tamataupe.

When Nita spent time with Ligeiro, Luisa started hanging out with me at the house. She was full of curiosity about life in the U.S. She asked endless questions and couldn't grasp (like many other Brazilians) why we would leave our homes to come and live like the other *matutos* (hillbillies) in the country. One day we were sitting on our bed talking. My bare feet were propped up in front of me and she touched the ball of one foot and sucked in her breath in surprise.

"Dona Ana," she exclaimed, "why are your feet so soft? Here, feel mine!" Hers were like leather from going barefoot constantly. The only time she and her sister or their mother wore shoes was to go to market in a distant town. And even then, they wore thongs (what we now call flip-flops).

> *Monday, Feb. 7–I bandaged Davina's hand again today. It's healing well. João Agosto's kids brought us a huge jaca fruit. Dan brought back five sacks of cement and tomorrow a truck is bringing some bricks for the garden construction project.*
>
> *This month's goals for me are:*
>
> *1-Help Dan plan an organizational meeting for the garden*
>
> *2-Teach 5 new stitches in embroidery class and start on hand towels*
>
> *3-Visit the training center in Carpina and plan a meeting in Buenos Aires with Sister Dulcina*
>
> *4-Discuss a contract with the Bishop*
>
> *5-Find a teacher for the school*
>
> *6-Start buying and making equipment for the school*
>
> *7-Weigh 5 children*
>
> *8-Write Dan's folks about building the school*
>
> *9-Make home visits and buy a saddle.*

Our home on the plantation was on a well-worn, dusty footpath that ran between several of the worker huts. One of the foremen for the cane crew had lived in it previously but the three-room house had been improved with a fresh coat of whitewash and a concrete floor. Inside, we could look up to the exposed rafters and see the clay tiles that formed the roof.

Outside the front door an immense mango tree dominated the landscape, and we learned to love the tart, peachy taste after a worker cut off a slice with his machete and gave us a sample. He advised us to suck the fruit rather than eat it, but I preferred to savor mine by chewing the flesh. We would eventually purchase an electric blender so we could make our own fruit *vitaminas* (we know them now as smoothies).

During the rainy season, the plantation sometimes flooded roads, keeping us prisoners until things dried up.

As you walked in through the Dutch door of our hut, you entered the main living area, a long room with one wooden window without a screen that remained open during the day. That room held our cardboard bookshelves, the rocking chairs (the one Dan loved so much grew a twin), and little else other than a few artisan leather stools. We decorated the walls with Brazilian wood carvings and a colorful batik we had purchased in Recife.

A large, narrow bedroom mirrored the living space and was accessible through a doorless entry where we hung a curtain. Another wooden window brought light into that room, which held a straw mattress on a rustic wooden frame with slats, a rough nightstand, and a wooden wardrobe.

The kitchen was at the back of the house. It held our kerosene refrigerator, kerosene stove, a table, and a waist-high clay water jug. A filtered clay water dispenser with a spout stood on a concrete counter that also held an enamel wash basin where I washed and drained dishes and utensils and prepped food.

On the outside wall of the kitchen, directly under the former termite nest, was a door that led to our privy, the largest on the plantation. Workers finished it a few months after we moved in. It boasted two rooms–one that featured a bathroom with a porcelain toilet and the second room was the shower room. We flushed the toilet with dirty dish water and took a shower with a handled bucket suspended over the middle of the shower stall.

We had every comfort we could have asked for in our plantation hut, certainly more than any other resident. We completed the picture of domesticity with the companion animals we had rescued or adopted—an orange tabby cat we named Gringo and a gray tiger-striped cat we called Samaka, after a Philippine gardening book that held instructions for raised beds. Then we inherited a large tuxedo cat we called Jaworski after the last name of the Peace Corps couple that gifted him to us upon returning to the States.

We didn't do much to celebrate the one-year anniversary of our Peace Corps service while on Tamataupe de Flores. We were both too busy trying to get something accomplished. Dan was attempting to have a water tank and a garden shed built on top of a hill. The tank would irrigate a community garden. He faced delay after delay in getting construction materials purchased and brought to the plantation, since he had to rely on the work trucks that were in use nearly every day in the cane fields.

I was busy teaching embroidery classes, visiting houses to introduce myself, and doing nutrition surveys and census counts. I quickly developed the goal of starting a school on the plantation, since the nearest one was 8 kilometers away in the tiny town of Oitero. My work was to be supervised by the Catholic bishop in the nearby town of Nazaré da Mata, but Brazilian bureaucracy dictated that we had to have the bishop sign an agreement first. That led to a series of meetings, missed appointments, and the same kinds of delays Dan faced with his garden project. Nothing happened fast in rural Northeast Brazil, and this became a source of constant frustration for the goal-and results-oriented American I was. (And still am.)

Wednesday, March 1–*Time is passing much faster. I haven't been bored for ages. I'm reading The Agony and The Ecstasy. What a book! The biggest flaw is that it doesn't show Michelangelo's works. Guess I'm just going to have to travel to Italy someday.*

Gringo is on my lap and a Peter, Paul and Mary album is playing on the tape deck. Dan is reading in the front room, and the rest of the world is shut out. Contentment. We could be in the States without much stretch of imagination. It's good to have a mental escape from this place occasionally.

We went to Nazaré this morning to meet with Marco (the Recife director of the Peace Corps) and the bishop. Marco left minutes before we got there. The bishop is going soon to talk with LBA (Legião Brasileira de Assistência—a social services agency operating on national lottery funds). I wonder how long this convênio (Memorandum of Understanding) making process is going to last?

I want to make a new term for embroidery classes and just have each class meet once a week. Bi-Bil, one of the students and a maid at the casa grande, didn't like that idea. She thinks two times a week isn't enough. I suggested the idea of a club and couldn't explain the concept very well. Bi-Bil thought the purpose would be to have parties. I talked to Marco (the plantation owner's son-in-law and the boss of this place) for a while this evening.

Dan's been a little depressed today. The cost estimate for his project was off a good deal and we have to buy more of everything. Luckily the trucks will be available. But my poor husband. He's going to suffer from mental exhaustion before that garden and water tank are finished. He's done so much running around and with so few results.

I'm gonna ride around the plantation on the mule with Ligeiro tomorrow or by myself if he can't go. I need to try and complete the visiting of homes before the meeting Tuesday night. Dan fell asleep in the rocker sitting up.

Sunday, March 12, 1972*—One year ago today we arrived in Brazil. How much we've gone through since then! Thank God we speak better Portuguese now than then.*

The Dutch-built church where we opened a pre-school.

-14-

COOPERATING WITH PLANTATION OWNERS

Our work on the plantation depended on communication and cooperation with the owners. Or at least their relatives.

Tamataupe de Flores' owner was one of the famed "Colonels" of Pernambuco history. Sr. Clovis lived with his European-blonde wife in a lush mansion in Recife. Over a holiday meal he invited us to that first year, he pointed to Dona Ione and bragged about his trophy wife and how he pampered her with clothes and jewelry. Everyone on the plantation knew that he kept a mistress in a small apartment near the red-light district and I'm sure Ione even knew about it and probably approved of it. The practice was just part of the culture.

Clovis and Ione had two daughters. Amira was married to Marco and Clovis tasked his son-in-law with managing Tamataupe. Seldom did Clovis or Ione show their faces at the *casa grande*. But Marco did, often spending several days, especially during the cane harvest, and sometimes bringing Amira.

We hadn't been at our job site very long before Amira left their beach house in Recife to come to the plantation with Marco to meet the Americans. She immediately took an interest in my work and wanted to help in any way she could. I would soon discover that her help came with strings that included doing things her way. She wanted to open a school in the old church but then became pregnant and preferred to stay in the city close to doctors. That often left me at a standstill with my work. And while we were friends, and she valued the opinions of an American, I knew there was a huge gulf between us culturally. I felt as if she regarded me as just another of her servants. Yet I could not have accomplished much on the plantation without her approval or help.

As we adjusted to living on a sugar cane plantation and tried to help improve the lives of the workers and their families, literacy became a stronger focus than improving nutrition through gardening projects and assessment of degrees of malnutrition. These children needed schooling that their parents had never received. They needed a way off of the plantation with its endless cycle of poverty and premature death.

My uphill trip to get a school established on the plantation was literal and figurative. With the help of Amira, we were able to start a type of pre-school aimed at giving plantation children basic skills like holding a pencil, forming a line, brushing teeth, and singing songs.

This pre-school or interim school grew out of our frustration with Brazilian educational bureaucracy and an interminable wait to get approval for hiring a state-paid teacher. Amira and I opened the school in the old church. It was an unlikely spot for a school. The first time the plantation overseer opened the doors to the side altar of the church I was assaulted by the stench of bat dung. The floor was covered with three inches, probably a century's accumulation of it. But I was young and stupid and immediately tackled sweeping it all out the back door with a homemade broom. In retrospect, I should have at least worn a carpenter's mask to protect my lungs.

At least one burial crypt was revealed underneath the bat dung, and it was caving in. But young and clueless me just positioned a table over the crypt and went about the business of making that side altar into a school room.

Getting the school operational, with Amira's help, kept my mind and my days occupied. Each day I descended the hill from our hut, walked across the pond dam at the bottom, and around cattle, then climbed the steep clay road to the church. Sometimes I made the trek twice in one day.

When the school first opened, I was overweight. By the time it had operated a few weeks, I had slimmed down considerably from climbing that hill.

The hills of Tamataupe de Flores were in fact the bane of my existence, as was that damn cattle pond. One night, at the beginning of the rainy season, we returned late from a trip to Recife and had to park the Jeep at the bottom of the hill and carry groceries and other items we had purchased in the city to our house. In the dark and the mud.

I was carrying my shoes and a sack of groceries as we slid in the mud, stepping around sleeping cattle. At one point in that trek, I was sure I had just stepped on a snake. At least it felt like a snake.

As we struggled up the steep, slippery hill to the house, I lost my hold on the grocery sack and spilled all the fresh green beans we had purchased earlier in the day.

That was it! I had a meltdown right there. I bawled and blamed Dan for the mess and for bringing us to this God-forsaken hell hole. The meltdown was driven by homesickness, helplessness, and fatigue. Dan just ignored my tirade and continued climbing that hill, leaving me to make my own way to the house.

Trying to get a school started on Tamataupe was my chief frustration. For Dan, it was getting any traction at all in building a community garden facility.

On the school front, two women from the *Nûcleo* (school certification center) came out to look over the church and they left both Dan and me depressed. For one thing, they were squeamish about the bats, the crypts, and the smell. They said these are not good conditions for a school and they acted quite pessimistic when told that Marco would furnish the missing tables. All the time we had the feeling they were laughing at us for living in the "jungle." They kept asking us if we liked it here. Why do people think we're crazy to love the country?

We filled in the waiting and boredom with lots of reading, mixed with some outright laziness. Some nights I did the dishes after a hastily-prepared meal, but on other occasions, I let them sit overnight to attract roaches.

One of us would go to bed early with a book to read, and to wait until the lights at the casa grande went off, meaning ours were extinguished as well.

No movies for us. No television. No conversations on the phone with friends. Sometimes I embroidered and once in a great while Rod and Dorothy were at our place, and we play a long, tiring game of pinochle. I always pooped out first.

Planning and organizing my embroidery and sewing classes served to energize me in those days on Tamataupe, giving me the illusion I could control something while I waited for things to happen with the school.

I had written letters to friends and relatives in the U. S. about our efforts to start a school on the plantation. On one trip back to Recife we arrived at the Peace Corps office to discover six letters had arrived, most of them good ones that renewed my admiration for humans. Kathy Fuhrman, a friend from journalism school, sent a $25 check for the school. Grandma Garrett and the Wakarusa Ladies Aid planned to send thread and seeds. Dan's Aunt Lois wanted to send money and Dan's mom wrote about sending a big package.

In a letter received from my mother, I learned she was not happy where they were living at Lake Pomme de Terre in Missouri. I couldn't say I blamed her. They had moved around so much and worked so hard and had so little to show for it.

Like organizing and list-making, I always felt good when I could rearrange our hut. We found a kitchen cabinet in Recife and brought it home. Stocking it and reorganizing the entire house kept me busy mentally and physically for a while. Besides, I needed to make more space for the sewing classes that were now being held in our hut. It was an almost endless task to keep embroidery thread organized and untangled, ready for the next class session.

And as much as I hated math in high school, I even found myself teaching math to two of the girls before having them work on embroidery. My students were so industrious and motivated to learn the stitches. I prepared small notebooks for them and each time they finished a little square of fabric with a new stitch, we glued them into notebooks so they'd have an example when they got ready for a larger project. Just a few weeks ago, I found my own sample embroidery notebook. It brought a flood of memories.

While we waited for approval to hire a schoolteacher and open the school, Amira and Marco waited for their first child. We heard a rumor one day on the plantation that she'd given birth and rushed to Recife to visit the new baby. But it was just gossip.

Eventually Amira had her boy by Caesarian, so we went back to Recife for a visit and to take a present. During the visit, Amira mentioned that because of "politics," there would be a delay in starting the school. That depressed me for the rest of the week.

By then I had 21 students in embroidery classes and had to turn away five girls because there was just not enough room to accommodate any more. Ica was one of the girls I turned away and felt so bad about it. She had 51 literacy students herself and taught morning, afternoon, and night. She hadn't been paid for six months. At night her adult students studied by lamplight because she had no electricity in her house. And I couldn't crowd in five more in my hut? What was I thinking?

When I wasn't teaching embroidery classes, I continued making home visits to assess malnutrition stages in the children. My legs got so tired from riding the plantation mule.

I'd picked up babies and they'd pee all over me because the poor kids didn't wear diapers. The families usually had at least one pig or goat that would walk behind the infants and clean up their messes.

The adults were also on my radar for health issues. Ze Salviano had worms and was unable to keep anything on his stomach. I advised his wife, Severina, to boil the drinking water and tried to explain how worms are transmitted. By then I was beginning to see the need for a privy campaign. I considered convincing the Salvianos to build a rustic one of bamboo and *palha* (palm fronds) to set a good example. But that never got off the ground.

On my home visits I heard a lot of gossip, including a story about a woman named Maria who was taking all kinds of teas and took five injections to try and abort her pregnancy. At the time I remarked, at least to myself, that it would be a miracle if that baby wasn't stillborn or born with deformities.

I continued to dress wounds and supply medicines on my home visits. And despite the many months of those visits, I only had 26 families surveyed for malnutrition. Out of those, there were 36 children of school age. Fourteen of the families had privies. I didn't ask how many actually used them. Most of them didn't have drainage holes—only a shaft leading outside and onto the ground.

On one of my mule trips around the plantation, I met José Flosino, the local Shangoa (similar to voodoo) expert. Both were big people and talked with a drawl. I imagined they were direct descendants of slaves. Sometimes late at night we could hear the Shangoa drums and were so curious about their rituals. But not curious enough to investigate. We had been warned about that.

-15-

THE VACCINE CAMPAIGN

While we were waiting for things to work through bureaucracies to start a school in the church, the health issues we witnessed gave us the impetus to start a vaccine campaign. We made a visit to the Hygiene Post in Nazaré da Mata to talk to three nurses about giving vaccines and were overwhelmed and surprised by their willingness to cooperate. They offered to give tetanus to adults and polio and DPT to children. We just needed to furnish transportation and feed them. They made plans to be at Tamataupe in the morning and at Bonito for Rod and Dorothy in the afternoon.

The problem then became convincing the people to get vaccinated. They were afraid. I was so disappointed in Luisa when she told me she didn't believe in them because they were unnatural; not God-given. I'm sure there were others who felt the same but were not willing to express it to us. We started to *campaign for the campaign* by holding a few public discussions and once again getting on that damn mule and riding around for home visits.

The day of the vaccines was one full of people, happenings, conversations, confusion, and fatigue.

Things were so unorganized. I couldn't get the church door unlocked and had to send for some water and to have the lights turned on. Everything combined to make us run around and sweat a lot. And there was so much noise and confusion from kids screaming and mothers shouting.

We vaccinated 150 people above five years old and 60-some below. Not a bad turnout. There were four nurses, a public health official, and the *motorista* for lunch. Marco got mad at me because I said there would be four people for lunch and there was not enough food.

So many things went wrong, and I kept lamenting the disorganization and worrying that the nurses were upset with us and wouldn't want to come again. But we did get a lot accomplished. Besides the vaccines, we weighed 41 kids. I kept seeing the smiles of those mothers. They seemed to be saying "thanks for taking an interest in my children."

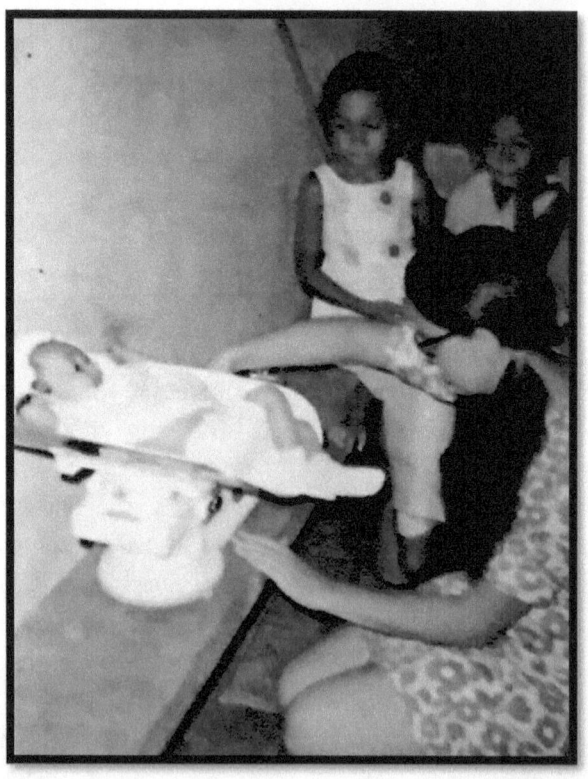

Weighing babies at the first vaccination campaign, Tamataupe.

In addition to the vaccine campaign, the girls on the plantation began pressuring me to teach *corte y costura* (cutting and sewing). I have no recollection of when I managed to purchase a treadle sewing machine and then teach myself to use it so I could turn around and teach them. But I had learned to sew in 4-H and home economics and was ambitious enough and poor enough the summer before Dan and I got married to make my own wedding dress, so I guess it wasn't that much of a leap to learn to sew on a machine powered by my foot instead of electricity.

The day the plantation girls started on the sewing machine was one of riotous laughter as some of them had a hard time making the pedal go. They initially thought they couldn't learn, but I assured them it was just a matter of practice. I tried to be patient as they got the bobbin tangled every week and broke many needles. One of the girls even put a needle through her finger.

Through all that learning curve, I still managed to keep my hands busy with other creative projects, including making a needlepoint purse, a skirt and dress for myself, and a crocheted baby blanket for Dan's brother's baby that was due in May. I also tried to get creative with my cooking, improvising new ways to fix the fresh vegetables we had access to whenever we got out for market. We also had our own garden in the yard.

That small garden of sweet corn, collards, and lettuce was looking pretty promising, until the day I found the snake. I was reaching for some collards and noticed a red and black diamond pattern in the weeds. I managed to pull my hand away just in time to avoid touching one of Brazil's most poisonous snakes. My heart was racing so fast from the fright, but I followed the snake's body with my eyes and located its head. Lucky for me its mouth was occupied trying to swallow a toad.

As for Dan's community garden project, the shed lacked a roof, floor, doors, and windows. But he had lost interest in trying to complete it, especially after talking with Marco. We began to think he was stonewalling Dan on the project, making up every excuse possible not to devote any manpower or transportation of supplies to it. So Dan decided to give up on the community garden and work on home gardens. Just like I lost interest in the garden when I found it occupied by a snake. But I did worry that Dan would not be happy if he went home without achieving his goal or finishing his work.

He didn't share my need to always stay busy or make up things to do to fill the hours. He seemed content to sit in the rocker and read all day. I wouldn't learn until decades later that some of his family members suffered from clinical depression. I think being powerless on the plantation caused him to be depressed, but he would never admit it.

Dan did make a big improvement in our hut, installing a screened ceiling, and moving the light fixtures lower. He did the ceiling after we got our fill of bug bites in our sleep. Something stung me under the eye, and I puffed up so much I couldn't get my glasses on. Then one Saturday night when Rod and Dorothy were staying with us, I happened to wake up and look for Gringo when my flashlight lit up a scorpion descending the wall by the bed mere inches from my legs.

As our work progress stalled, Dan and I tried to stay on top of happenings back in the States. We bought a shortwave radio and put up an antenna so Dan could listen to BBC News. We also bought *Time* magazine at Recife newsstands every chance we got. George Wallace had been shot and the Pentagon bombed. We learned through letters that Dan's siblings were planning a big celebration for their parents' silver anniversary. Oh, how we longed to be home then! It was such a fabulous time of year in Missouri. If it weren't for *The Lord of the Rings,* I'd probably have pulled out my hair as I was torn between the Southern and Northern hemispheres. The adventures in the land of Hobbits, dwarves, elves, wizards, and ents allowed me to escape my homesickness.

It also helped our moods to start planning what we would do with our lives when we got back home. At one point Dan and I got excited about talking to George, a former volunteer, about a university on a ship. But that pursuit soon slipped from our minds, even though I had been determined to write for information.

During a stasis in our activities, our state Peace Corps director surprised us with a visit. He came to tell us the contract with the bishop for the school had been approved and had been sent to Rio for final national approval. He suggested we talk to Dona Anita

Aline, the head of the Brazilian lottery, and find out what we needed to do until the money got released. He thought that would be in July, but I had my doubts.

We showed our director the church and the water tank and shed. After he left, I decided to do something to the church to make it look less bare.

And suddenly, it was time for a second vaccine campaign. We had a poor turnout due to the weather and people's memories of the way the first one hurt.

Despite all my activities and accomplishments, I often gave into depression myself. One of my journal entries from those days shocks me now.

> *I hate this God-forsaken place today. Is it asking too much to have a school for these poor kids? It's not even my responsibility, so why am I taking it on myself and worrying so much? What are we doing here? Reading The Zin-Zin Road is not helping my mood. We should have gone to Africa.*
>
> *When I step outside, I see weeds waist high, no flowers in the flowerpots, weeds in the collards and radishes, and trash in the yard. The state of our life right now is like our yard.*
>
> *But I don't want to go home, especially before we've done something. Rod and Dorothy are definitely leaving Bonito—either to the States or another Brazilian state. People are stealing things from the garden there and they feel they're wasting their time.*
>
> *Over 11 months to go; actually, ten if we terminate in May to travel.*

Following that journal entry, I decided to make a list of what we had accomplished on Tamataupe.

> • *I've taught about 35 girls to embroider and am*

teaching ten to sew on the machine.

- *We're about to get a school functioning.*
- *We've saved a man's life, bought lots of medicine and supported his family. We've bought medicine for several other families and probably saved a baby's life.*
- *We've helped two or three men retire and get pensions.*
- *We've given the people some diversions by showing films in the church.*
- *We've had several children and adults vaccinated for whooping cough, tetanus, and polio.*
- *We've loaned people books and bought several books for their use, at least the few here who are literate. We've also talked to them and sympathized with their problems.*
- *We've given out a few packets of vegetable seeds.*
- *We've built Marco a nice water tank and added on to his stable, even though that was not the original goal.*

Then we began discussing and debating what else we could do with our time in Brazil. That called for another list.

- *Dan could help people with their home gardens and do some small animal projects. He could also supervise a privy project.*
- *We could improve the church building for a school, cement the floor, build a bathroom, paint the windows. We could arrange for literacy classes.*
- *I could teach more embroidery and sewing classes and teach craft classes. I could try to get a women's club going.*
- *We could teach English classes in Buenos Aires as well as try to start a public library and train midwives.*
- *Dan could maybe help Mike Morris in his co-op work in this area.*

That all sounded like it could keep us busy and be satisfying work, but I wondered if I could convince Dan or myself. I didn't really want to leave. Like our director had pointed out, we were the only volunteers left on any *engenho*, and none will come after us. We began thinking it would be better to do the best we could and hope that the little help we gave would not be futile or forgotten.

Our toughest job in our volunteer work on the plantation had been getting over the rough spots, the boredom, frustration, and the feeling that we were two ants fighting against the hopeless forces of poverty, ignorance, hunger, and sickness with little money, organization. or moral support behind us. Like Dan often said, there aren't many people who could have done what we were doing.

-16-

THE SCHOOL OPENS WITHOUT A STATE TEACHER

Amira came to an embroidery class one day and in just a few hours she decided that she and I are going to start the school Monday after next, teaching motor skills to smaller children (ages five to ten) so that they'll be ready for learning when and if a teacher comes.

Friday was enrollment and by Monday I was buying supplies and running off some exercises on the mimeograph at the Peace Corps office in Recife. Then the rest of the week was devoted to getting the church ready—whitewashing the walls, fixing the roof leaks, and cementing the floor. We planned to put up bookshelves and a screen in the back room to keep supplies in. We planned two sessions to accommodate all the kids, one from 8 a.m. to 10 a.m. and one from 10 a.m. to noon.

We held a mother's meeting for the school and it started off poorly. It was to be in the church, but the key was locked in the *casa grande* and Marco had the key. He got mad the previous night when he caught the gardener in his liquor cabinet, and said he wouldn't trust anyone with any of his keys.

The day was pretty rainy but could have been worse. There were actually two meetings because the mothers came at different times, but it was better that way. I told them when classes would start, what kids were in which class, showed them an apron, gave them sample "report cards," and repeated major points of importance. There were a few problems with brothers and sisters being in different classes, but I think we resolved the difficulties somehow.

119

I liked watching the women interact. They gave each other stiff, formal handshakes instead of kissing both cheeks like richer Brazilian women do. And even these poor women had cliques and petty jealousies and feuds, but the day they knew a school was opening they shared a common bond. Being without a school for three years made them realize how important it is.

We had 38 kids enrolled, would accept no more than 40. I began using my sewing machine to make student aprons and embroider them with the name of the school, labeled water cups, made name tags, and cut file folders. It felt so good to be busy and excited again.

When the first day of school arrived, I thought it was going to be terrible with the kids not able to understand me tripping all over my tongue. But it was fun. First, they learned how to pray *"Menino Jesus, olhai por nos, hoje, amanhá e sempre,"* (Little Boy Jesus, look after us today, tomorrow, and always) and then how to make the sign of the cross. The poor kids had never done it and were doing it on their cheeks and mouths—anywhere but the right places. Then we sang *"Bom Dia."* Almost everyone sang. They liked music.

I explained how they must act in the school and what kinds of things we would be doing. Then I taught them to form a line and march outside. Done! That was all for the day.

They all seemed so relieved that they didn't get a vaccine.

Friday, July 14–I didn't do so well in class today. But I'm still elated about teaching. It's such a challenge but so wearing on the nerves, and it will only get worse as the kids get over the novelty of school. Still, it's fun and like learning to be a child all over again.

I was planning my lesson for Tuesday when I remembered how we used to trace around our hands in kindergarten. I included that in my plans. It may be too advanced for their motor skills, but it will be interesting to see the results.

I read Little Red Riding Hood to them, but it was hard

to keep their attention. They were all tired. Moacir slept on a bench during Amira's class. And José de Lima didn't have any problem adjusting to his new seat. Right away he gave Lindacir a big kiss. He's a bit of a problem and thinks he can be the exception to the rule and not participate. He never prays or sings. When I'm firm with him he smarts off. Antonio is another one who doesn't participate. But his problem is shyness. He cries every day.

***Wednesday, July 26**–Amira isn't here this week so I'm teaching two classes. It's satisfying but tiring. So much work goes into preparing for class. And I always worry that I'm cross with the kids. Today we played Lion Hunt and learned some new songs. I wish I knew some Brazilian games to teach them. Maybe we'll try Drop the Handkerchief.*

Samaka wasn't at home all day today. Finally, Joséfa the cook came by and said the cat was at the casa grande and wouldn't let anyone catch her. I went down and got her and carried her home. The poor, sweet thing must've followed me to school.

***Wednesday, August 2**–What is it with Amira? The last few days I haven't been able to stand her. She stayed a few minutes for class (mine) and corrected me in front of my students. I get so nervous when she's there. Then last night she fired Luisa, mostly because of Bi-Bil, who hadn't done the baby's wash like she'd promised Luisa. Also, Luisa used a box of soap in one day and Amira thought that was wasteful, although Bi-Bil scrubbed two bathroom floors and Zephina washed out some towels out of the same box.*

Amira stayed for all of my class today and I wasn't so nervous. I did okay despite her interruptions for suggestions about who could be the butterfly in the Christmas program. Then she compared my students' cards with hers and kept saying mine were bad, forgetting that my kids are much younger. Then she came up with the idea of giving catechism classes so the kids can take first communion. Splendid! It's bad enough being tied up every morning, but every afternoon too?!

My relationship with Amira was one of me being like a favorite, well-educated maid. Despite all the excitement and togetherness of opening the school, I felt no closer to her than I did upon meeting her.

I did have one thing to thank her for. She gave me so much instruction on how to teach school and taught me so much about the culture. Also, my Portuguese improved considerably working with her. But in the end, I began to long for the simple ways of the *matuta* (Brazilian hillbilly) women. At least they didn't look down on me.

PART V:

A HOME IN TOWN

-17-

ANOTHER MOVE - THIS TIME TO CIVILIZATION

Almost immediately after we opened the pre-school in the church, we made plans to move off the plantation. We would be relocating to Carpina, a town larger than Nazaré and a lot closer to Recife. Dan went to Recife to talk to the owner of a house we found in a perfect location with land and trees around it.

We already had a three-day vacation to Natal, a beautiful city on the coast a few hours bus ride north of Recife. We stayed with a volunteer friend, Rick Lawless, and toured the Ship Hope, went to the beach and an old fort. We even called Dan's parents from Natal, and it seemed like we were calling from Columbia, Missouri. No one knew what to say. They all sang Happy Birthday to me, and we told them we'd like to buy the Braymer newspaper when we get home. I'm sure they were confused about what we're going to do because every week it changed.

Back on the plantation, we had given up any hope of getting through educational bureaucracies to get a state teacher. No one wanted to teach on an *engenho,* especially one so far from civilization. Rather than end my classes, I asked Albertina to teach them, and planned to pay her 30 cruzeiros a month for four months. By that time there would be no more money in our school fund and the problem would be Amira's. I had a long talk with Albertina after class one day, mostly about the living conditions at Tamataupe.

A lot of people were upset about our impending departure. They didn't have anyone else to turn to when they were in a tough spot and needed transportation or medicine. Everyone wanted to leave, but for those who had lived here all their lives and didn't have an education, it was next to impossible to live in the street (*rua*) as they called the city.

Albertina lamented the sugarcane planted up to their doorstep with no space to plant beans or vegetables. She also mentioned the water problem. The one good water hole near her house was filled with insecticide that somehow got there when workers were treating the cane. My heart ached for them all.

I filled the remaining days on the plantation continuing to help as many people as possible, including Joséfa, who had "adopted" an orphaned baby and asked for some material to make clothes for it. It got me in a giving-away mood. I gave Carminha an ugly pink dress Mother sent and Donna Severina some GERAN surveys for her grandchildren to write on. I started giving the girls in my class some old dresses and shoes, knowing that other women and girls would flock to the door of our hut asking for *lembranças* (souvenirs).

Our Peace Corps life got a rejuvenating shot of purpose when we both got new assignments and moved off the sugar cane plantation. I made plans to establish a Head Start-type program in the small town of Trachunhaem, a town populated with workers who made clay products like large water pots and cooking utensils. The town boasted a church, brick streets, and was located just off the highway between Carpina and Nazaré da Mata.

It worked out beautifully that we would live in Carpina, a much larger town, and I would commute to Trachunhaem while Dan would work in the town of Limoeiro with an agricultural cooperative run by Italian priests. My pre-school would be financed with Brazilian lottery funds and overseen by the bishop of Nazaré, whom I had already been working with on the school project at Tamataupe.

When we determined where we would live, the search began for a house in Carpina. Several houses were rented out from under us just as we inquired about the property. Finally, we located a white stucco house just a block from a service station which served as a main bus stop on the route to Recife. The home was a mansion compared to our hut on the plantation. Situated on an unpaved street, the property featured a stuccoed brick wall in the front, with a gate that opened onto a wonderful surprise—a patch of yard covered in thick grass. The old man who lived in a mud hut next door was the caretaker and we paid him to keep the lawn clipped, a task he performed while kneeling and using a pair of hand clippers.

The town of Tracunhaem was already an established community of ceramics (clay) artists who made clay statutes as well as more practical clay cooking utencils.

Our rental house featured a front porch with beautiful floor tiles and the front door opened to a large living room. That front room led to an open dining room which had double wood doors that opened to a back porch covered with a clay tile roof. A large concrete laundry tub took up one corner of the porch. The expansive back yard held several mature fruit trees—cashew, mango, orange, lime, and avocado. Each July that dirt back yard became littered with rotting fruit that fell from high up in those tall trees, as we had no ladder tall enough to reach the fruit. Sometimes we were able to shake the trees to give up their fruit.

Our housing got a big upgrade when we moved to the small city of Carpina with an indoor bathroom and running water.

Back inside the house, to the right of the living room, was a bedroom and to the left, a small room that became my craft, music, and sewing room. We were elated to have an indoor bathroom with a working heated shower (if you can call a shower head with a bare electric wire heating the water as it came out of the head a heated shower).

Instead of wooden shutters opening the house to the outside, our new house boasted jalousie, crank-out windows with opaque glass leaves.

With this new house we had landed ourselves solidly in the Brazilian middle class. It may not have been copacetic with our Peace Corps leaders in Recife, especially when paired with the illegal Jeep parked in front of the house, but by then, after being shuttled to two different plantations and living in a Recife hotel for a few months, they were not about to make much of a stink about us not living like peasants. Besides, the roles we each took on with our new jobs merited a little bit better living conditions.

We brought our simple furniture from Tamataupe, adding a red vinyl couch in the front room, and what passed for a coffee table.

And of course, we decorated walls with Brazilian batiks and wood carvings, adding decorative clay pottery and statues we began acquiring from the artisans in Trachunhaem.

I soon adopted Brazilian housecleaning methods, especially when mopping the ceramic tile floors. That involved pouring water on the floors or running a hose from the outside hydrant and hosing the floors down, adding a little dish soap, bringing in a broom to swish and scrub, followed by a squeegee to push the water and suds out the back door. The final touch was taking a large rag or towel and using my feet to sop up the excess, usually while playing some Brazilian or American music on our cassette tape player. I especially enjoyed the James Taylor tape a family member had sent us in a care package and "Mud Slide Slim" became my go-to mopping tune.

A big plus in the move to Carpina, besides living closer to "civilization" and Recife, was easier access to our friends and even neighbors. Noemia and Paulo lived across the street from us in Carpina. A childless couple in their late 40s or 50s (we never asked), they unofficially adopted us, taking us out to eat at area restaurants or inviting us over to dinner at their house, and to watch Brazilian soap operas on their television.

We were also closer now to our Mennonite volunteer friends, Karen and Bob. Dan and Bob often worked together on co-op projects, especially chicken and rabbit-raising projects. Bob and Karen were from Iowa and would eventually return to Mt. Pleasant, Iowa where Bob became a bank executive. But while we were all in Brazil, we often ate suppers together and Karen and I frequently collaborated on concocting Brazilian dishes that could be converted into American-tasting ones.

⌣•⌣

18

THE CINEMA THAT BECAME
A PRE-SCHOOL

My original plans to open a school on the plantation were transplanted to the town of Trachunhaem. I had several meetings with Anita Aline, the head of the Brazilian Assistance League (LBA), an organization funded by the federal lottery. I had originally met her while at Tamataupe. We finally got through all the paperwork and bureaucracy to sign an agreement that had the bishop of Nazaré continue oversight of this new project, with a side agreement by the city government.

The mayor of Trachunhaem, Sr. Pedro, was a brown, skinny man of about 50. If attention deficit disorder had been a thing back in the 1970s, he would have been diagnosed with it. This bundle of energy talked rapidly, changed the subject frequently, and made grandiose promises of cooperation with the American, emphasizing his talks with wild hand and arm gestures. We would eventually become good friends and even celebrate Carnaval together.

The first time we met, Sr. Pedro took us on a tour of Trachunhaem, bragging about all the good things he had done for the city since he'd been in office. He whisked us in his *rural* to a screeching stop in front of a dingy-colored stucco building supported by white pillars and surrounded by an honest-to-God moat. It reminded us of the futuristic architecture in the Brazilian capital of Brasilia. The sign on the front of the building shouted *CINE TEATRO*, or cinema theater, but it was evident it had not been used much to show motion pictures. We soon learned it was largely a party house, the scene of drunken dances and Trachunhaem's version of a country club. We were going to start a pre-school in it.

Carnaval (what we know as Mardis Gras in the States) is a huge celebration in Brazil. We celebrated for the first time with Peace Corps staffer José and his wife, and volunteer Gene and his wife Penha.

The cinema theater in Tracunhaem became a pre-school

until a new center could be built.

I soon began daily bus trips back and forth to the small village, met with city officials, made plans, and hired two teachers and two cooks. This center would be patterned after the Head Start program that was operating in the States under the umbrella of ACTION, the same agency that now administered Peace Corps and VISTA. And even as we opened the school in the old cinema, we made plans and started soliciting funds to build a permanent school. I also started organizing craft and cooking classes for the parents of the pre-school children.

Glaucidete Lopes was the first teacher I hired. A short, bubbly young woman with long, dishwater blonde hair, she exuded enthusiasm and love for the children. She never raised her voice, got cross, or showed an ounce of impatience, except for her fellow teacher and cousin, Zenilda.

I had quite a bit of sympathy for Zenilda because she had been raised by her single mother. She was tall and dark in contrast to Glaucidete's short roundness, and much more reserved. But I soon discovered, even with my limited grasp of Portuguese, she was a master of sarcasm. I would also fall for her many attempts to get a rise out of me, pushing me to exhibit my own impatience, even anger. It amused her to manipulate others, but she did her job well and followed my orders as her supervisor. She just had to complain and whine sometimes.

Dezinha and Finha Nova served as our cooks. Both were tall women in stature and hard workers, but as different from each other as Glaucidete and Zenilda. Dezinha was big boned and jolly, laughing and teasing her way through a workday. Finha Nova was slender and much more reserved but exuded a calm assurance that drew friends to her side. Both women worked at the school every day fixing lunches that usually included soups fortified with locally-purchased vegetables and bulgor or rice from USAID commodities distributions. Sometimes they fixed a sweet rice pudding or a grated corn dish sprinkled with cinnamon. The children relished whatever they prepared, as they often arrived with empty stomachs and returned home to meager suppers.

Finha Nova (left) and Dezinha were our cooks at the pre-school and came
to our house in Carpina once a week to do our laundry.
They even served as bartenders at a final party we held at our house.

    With the help of the teachers and cooks, we got the pre-school
established and running smoothly. I sometimes taught the children
but turned my attention to working with the students' mothers,
establishing a cooking class for them and eventually craft classes.

Presenting diplomas at an exposition to women and girls who completed
craft classes as members of our girls and women's clubs. The Catholic
bishop who supervised my work was present, as was the mayor,

Sr. Brito, and his wife, Dona Elena.

With the pre-school running smoothly, it was time for us to take a two-month leave back to the U.S. We had been in Brazil for two years, the normal length of Peace Corps service, and were required to take a leave.

But even though our work in Brazil was going well in the new location, we found it difficult to return after being back home. We were treated like royalty by family and friends while in Missouri. And we stuffed ourselves with all the fast food we loved but also enjoyed our parents' prepared meals.

By then my mother and stepfather and two youngest brothers had moved to a single-wide trailer after living a few years in a single-story building that had once been a large chicken house on 135th Street in Grandview. That's where they were living when Dan and I got married. I don't think Mother was happy about being back in a "white trash" trailer. My stepdad was managing a marina at Lake Pomme de Terre in central Missouri, brother Rick was pumping marine gas and was sometimes assisted by younger brother Tommy, and Mother worked in the small marina café. While visiting them at the lake, Dan and I enjoyed boat rides and getting to see my oldest brother, Jim, who had returned from Vietnam, along with his new wife and baby. They were living in Texas. We also enjoyed a boat ride and visit with my best friend from high school, Chris, her husband, and their toddler son.

Dan's Aunt RoseLee owned a dress shop in his hometown of Hamilton, and I spent quite a bit of my Peace Corps allowance on a new wardrobe that was better suited to the tropics than what I initially took to Brazil. Dan's cousin and RoseLee's daughter had played the flute in high school and since it was just lying around unused, I asked if I could borrow it. I had played the flute in junior high and thought I could teach myself to play again in Brazil. The flute got packed in our return trip luggage.

We had fun attending an auction where more of my Peace Corps allowance went to purchasing some beautiful pieces of antique furniture that would be used to set up a house when we returned to the States after our work was done in Brazil. Until that time, the furniture was stored in Dan's parents' house in a room that once functioned as a dining room but was much too small for their large family.

While in Missouri we also returned to our college campus for a visit with Dan's former roommates, who were still living there, and had a fabulous time without responsibilities or stressing about bureaucratic challenges in a third world country. But duty beckoned. I had a school to build, and Dan had lots of responsibilities with his agriculture co-op. On the way back to Brazil to finish our work and our third year of service in the Peace Corps, we stopped in Washington, D.C. to help with a "staging" for new volunteers. Our status as seasoned Peace Corps volunteers led to helping staff and trainers in Brazil also.

Upon our return, we jumped immediately back into the hectic schedule that was so foreign to Brazilians but second-nature to at least one American.

19

GETTING BACK INTO THE FLOW
OF VOLUNTEER WORK

Soon after we returned to our home in Northeast Brazil, we held a dinner in Trachunhaem for the mothers who had completed the cooking classes begun before our leave. It had a profound psychological effect on me. In fact, I considered it a turning point in my community development work.

Both of us had experienced difficulties in getting back into the groove of Brazil. I was further frustrated by a training session in community action sponsored by LBA. I discovered my work had been done without proper direction or plans. And here I had thought I was so organized with my lists! As Nininha, (pronounced nee-neen-ya) the daughter of the mayor, expressed, it was *"uma coisa jogada,"* a thrown-together thing. Worse yet was the fact that there had been little participation of the community in the project. I'd been doing it all myself.

Since that training, I had been in mental and emotional turmoil. Until the dinner.

I don't know why, but I'd been dreading the event before we even left for the States. Maybe I was giving heed to what everyone says about these people; that in the hour of work, everyone but a few would disappear and would expect to receive their diplomas and presents without lifting a hand. But that wasn't the case at all. The thing was a success, in spite of me being a nervous wreck all weekend because the Jeep broke down and upset the schedule.

Everyone was waiting on me to bring food and go pick up serving plates. By the time Sunday evening rolled around, I was almost screaming. At six o'clock I was still typing my speech, and at 6:20 I painted my nails, a Brazilian prerequisite for any special occasions.

Dan didn't help things a bit. He was so surly and didn't care at all about going. Once the thing started, however, all my worries and nerves dissolved. Maybe it was because of the type of people present—unpretentious, simple people.

For once, my hands didn't tremble when I gave my speech, or rather read it, as was the custom there, even with the President. It was a simple, enjoyable event, although far from perfect. The slip ups we made weren't that noticeable, and everyone seemed to enjoy themselves, especially the men. It led me to think that it might not be so hard to get them to come to meetings.

That dinner was an event that broke the ice in Trachunhaem. The women learned they could plan and execute an activity. And the men were beginning to show more of an interest in the project. That very week I resolved to solicit more community participation and scheduled a meeting with a group of mothers to plan the center's activities. I wanted to organize them as a sort of board of directors.

While I was getting the mothers organized, things were progressing with the operation of the pre-school in the current building, even as a new school was on the drawing board. An agreement for the new building had been signed by the bishop and returned to Rio for release of money. I contracted a carpenter to make the center's furniture and Sr. Pedro worked to have water installed and paint the center. We wanted to be ready by Inauguration Day on December 4.

Dan began to get busy with the cooperative. He'd already figured out a formula for hog ration and helped the co-op out of a tight spot by taking a broken motor into Recife for repair. He also started coordinating various projects to provide financial sustenance and planned to participate actively in a colonization project, if it ever got off the idealistic drawing board of the Italian priests who prepared it.

To add to the intensity of activities, we started planning to build a new grade school in Trachunhaem in addition to the pre-school.

Dan spent an entire day making a school blueprint and working out cost estimates while I wrote up the request and typed it at the Peace Corps office.

As always, there were many little worrisome moments, like the times Dan didn't come home from Recife.

Journal entry, November 3–It's nearly 2 a.m. and Dan is not home yet. He left for Recife at 8 this morning and said he'd be home early if he could. I made cookies this evening and waited to surprise him, but by 9 p.m. I went ahead and ate something. I wasn't too worried. He's been late before and usually had a good reason, invariably Jeep trouble. I played solitaire and tried to get some sleep, but now I'm almost sick. I try to imagine all the things that could have happened. At this point, I won't even care if he went to the Zona (red light district) as long as he's alive. I keep picturing that horrible train crossing where we came so close to being killed. There's nothing to do but wait until morning. If he's not back by 7, I'm getting on the bus for Recife.

It would be so much easier at home. I'd just phone the places where I thought he might have been. That failing, I'd call the police. I should prepare myself for the worst. Otherwise, if something's happened, I'll go to pieces. Without at least mental and emotional preparation, I'll still go to pieces.

Only four more hours till daylight. Guess I'd better get some sleep. If only the horrible feeling in my stomach would go away.

I don't recall now what kept Dan from coming home that night. He didn't have an accident, thank God! He may have missed the bus and spent the night behind the Peace Corps office. There was just no way back then to communicate such situations. But that always made me anxious with worry and the frequent lack of control we had over our lives in Brazil. The only antidote was our youth and our ability to roll with the problems.

We were guests in this country. And while we were there to help and serve, it never got easy or comfortable. Installing and supervising a pre-school in a municipal building provided many opportunities for further lessons in patience and flexibility.

By Christmas Eve that year I was so busy I didn't have time to look at the calendar and wish the little squares could be crossed off sooner. Five days a week, I was at the center. It officially opened December 11 but was functioning rather minimally. The furniture hadn't arrived, so we borrowed tables and chairs from the mayor's office—not very suitable as they were too high for kids to sit at comfortably. What we desperately needed were storage cabinets. Sr. Pedro owed the carpenter money and as soon as he got it, he planned to buy paint and Formica and other materials to finish up. Since his candidate to replace him as mayor had won the election by only nine votes, Sr. Pedro now seemed disinterested and bitter. Not once did he ask about the grade school project.

One Sunday there was a dance in the center, so we had to take down wall decorations and lock all the toys and kitchen utensils in the storage room. Monday, when I arrived for class, the place was a disaster—charcoal on the kitchen floor, leftover food, beer bottles, broken glass, vomit in my office, and the men's bathroom was indescribable. Not until Tuesday afternoon was it completely cleaned. On Monday, we called off classes.

Sr. Pedro said there would never be another party there during his term. Then his daughter told me they wanted to move our center to the school. I prepared for a fight about that. The girls didn't want to teach there saying it was hot, small, and not centrally located. Besides, during the school term there would be evening classes in the building, and the boys were notorious for their destructiveness.

The week of the holidays we had simple Christmas parties for the kids–a *quebra panela* (Brazilian version of a piñata), Christmas songs and stories and cake, bananas and juice for refreshments. We hung stockings for each child with a comb and a toothbrush inside. That was the only Christmas present a lot of them would get. I took lots of pictures.

The first year the center operated in Tracunhaem, I introduced a nativity scene for the Christmas program.

That Christmas season was much more enjoyable for Dan and me personally than the last. Rod and Dorothy sent us a small artificial Christmas tree from the States, complete with ornaments and tinsel. I hung Christmas cards over the doorway at our house in Carpina. Aunt Lois sent us each a paperback book. I bought Dan a notebook and a comb and brush set—not what I wanted to get him, but what he needed.

On Christmas Day we traveled to a volunteer family's house on the beach for a feast. We had a turkey dinner at the Peace Corps office prior to that, for which we made dozens of Christmas cookies. Everyone marveled at them. Dan's ingenuity amazed me. We had no cookie cutters, so he improvised.

We ended the holidays with a fun party at Gene Sanner's, a fellow volunteer who had married a Brazilian girl and stayed in the country. Dan danced himself crazy, and he wasn't even drunk. There were just some good old records—The Supremes, Aretha, Creedence, Beatles—and they brought back so many memories of college days.

20

PRE-SCHOOL INAUGURATED – MORE PROJECTS MATERIALIZE

I felt so good on New Year's Day, I couldn't believe it was the morning after a New Year's Eve party. But then it hit, and it hit both of us. It must have been a combination of the fish and *sarapatel* (a dish made with pork and pork viscera and curdled blood) we ate at the party. Dona Noemia gave me some medicine that took effect immediately. We went out to lunch with them, and I was able to eat quite a bit. Dan spent most of the meal in the restroom and then hardly touched his plate. We bought some medicine then and he got better while I got worse.

The party that made us so sick took place with our Brazilian friends from Trachunhaem. At midnight, there were so many hugs and kisses we felt awkward at times. Sr. Pedro made sure everyone's glass was full, and several times I had to put my hand over mine to prevent him from filling it up with vodka. I almost got sick from mixing champagne, eggnog, and vodka. We danced a lot, so I must have sweated the booze out. I was hoping the fact that both of us got sick wasn't an indication of how the rest of the year would play out.

On January 9, Sr. Brito, Trachunhaem's new mayor, came over to talk about the pre-school construction. I was a little intimidated by him as he was almost the opposite of Sr. Pedro, and not nearly as friendly. Fortunately, we resolved a lot of things. We decided on the tile for the floors, the type of windows, and more or less the time a bricklaying course I'd proposed for the local ceramics workers would begin. He agreed to accept Nininha as my substitute, paying her whatever she'd accept, but said requisitioning her from the state would be next to impossible. Luckily, he didn't want to put his wife,

Dona Elena, in my place. He said she couldn't even take care of him, let alone a school. That had been my worst fear. Brazilian politicians had a habit of rewarding their family members with good jobs.

Dona Noemia came over later that afternoon and we made a tea ring and did yoga. Dan got home at 10 and brought the *rural* and told me the story about how José's boss had been kidnapped as he left the Peace Corps office Tuesday. Three men had been hiding in the back of his car and took him to Dos Irmaões, (a rough neighborhood in Recife) stripped him, cut him, and put a gun in his mouth. He finally gave them his money. And to think this happened in broad daylight in front of our office! Everyone is scared now.

When we first arrived in Brazil we were surprised at the signs of crime, or crime deterrents, especially in Recife. The better homes were built like compounds, surrounded by high brick walls with driveways closed off by heavy wrought iron, locked gates. The one thing that always surprised us the most was the broken shards of glass that covered nearly every inch of the tops of those walls.

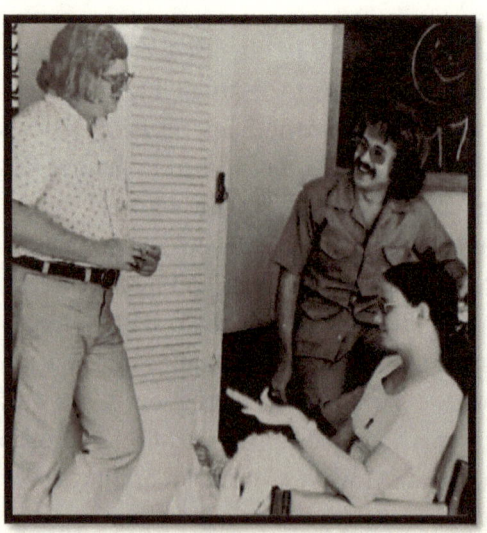

At the Recife Peace Corps office talking to a fellow volunteer.

Our Recife Peace Corps office was in one such compound. The mansion in the middle of the compound had been converted entirely to office space. But because so many people were coming and going into the offices, the driveway's metal gates were seldom closed. Still, it was a total shock to have our director robbed and kidnapped in broad daylight. The robbers must have been desperate, like so many of the poor people in Northeast Brazil.

January 14–I took a wad of cash out of the bank this morning to pay for the school refrigerator and material for kid's uniforms. Then I went to Senhor Pedro's to talk to Ninha. She didn't say much when I told her Sr. Brito had agreed to pay her to take charge of the school. I wonder if she's still doubtful about something.

The construction at the new pre-school isn't going very fast. They lined the outhouse this week but keep taking bricklayers off for other jobs.

The crochet class didn't go very well today. I was clumsy and impatient. I talked to Josias, our part time gardener, and we decided to go ahead and plant a few things in an old garden site to provide vegetables for school lunches, since the new garden hasn't been planted or planned yet.

This evening I started reading And Quiet Flows the Dawn.

January 21–It seems that the only time I write in this journal is when I'm depressed or melancholy. Then I usually read part of what I've written and laugh at the bad times and the stupid things I recorded. It makes me feel like we've come a long way. I know I'm a different person than I was two years ago. The biggest plus is that I take things much easier now and have more fun. The pace of life here is good for me.

The center is running so smoothly, that I'm just waiting for something disastrous to occur, like LBA telling me to redo the reports and get a fiscal note from the carpenter. I still have more furniture to paint but it looks so much better without those ugly brown chairs.

Friday's mother's meeting was a success. Eighty women attended. We signed up 50 for cooking and embroidery classes and will hold another registration meeting this Friday.

Today was the first Sunday we've spent at home in ages. We loafed and relaxed, Dan in the hammock strung between avocado trees and me in the rocker on the back porch. I finally finished my perpetual knitting and started a tapestry pillow. I should finish it in a few days. As always, I have to keep my hands busy with something creative.

The center will be inaugurated Sunday.

Construction begins on the new pre-school center.

It rained intermittently the day of the inauguration, but the proceedings went on. I had to give a speech and of course I was shaking, and I made a big Portuguese blooper by saying "pioneering temptation" instead of "pioneering effort."

The lunch for all the dignitaries went smoothly, but it was touch and go for a while. That morning no one knew what to do, or how to make those fancy dishes, (Brazilians are famous for decorating their dishes with food flowers, etc.) but it all turned out fine. Our Peace Corps director even came from Recife and brought his wife and two new volunteers.

The new agreement with LBA still needed to be drawn up but my motivation was lacking. I wasn't prepared to think about new projects or act on them and began to worry that I wasn't committed enough to my job and to integrating myself into the culture. We were keeping a distance between our American selves and our Brazilian identities. My job had become something to keep me busy all day and help the time go by. Perhaps I was beginning to feel the results of the impermanence of our situation in Brazil and the transience in our relationships.

That weekend a researcher picked our brains to find out what made volunteers well adjusted. Funny that after he left, I began to feel maladjusted.

Journal entry, February 10–Another dull Sunday with Dan in the hammock and me inventing things to do. I always seem to get inspired while doing the dishes. This evening, I realized that our experiences here have widened us in many ways. I was thinking how much more background I have now for creativity. If I ever take an art class, I'll have many more themes to draw on, and certainly enough to write about to fill a book. After reaching these conclusions, I drew three pictures of flowers and worked on a sketch of a little boy with his tin can pull toy. Children are hard to draw. Also, flute etudes are going through my head. I've been practicing the same ones for days.

By the second week of February, we had passed the milestone of the first day of pre-school classes in the new term. Things went fairly smoothly, but one of the children threw up.

At a meeting of the parents that week the men seemed uninhibited, and it turned into a lively discussion of cooperatives. They weren't sure what a cooperative was, but they wanted some easy way to sell their ceramics products and to borrow money. They obviously had no inkling of all the problems and details involved. We did create a commission to discuss the possibilities. Soon after that meeting, conversations started buzzing all over Trachunhaem. What was important about this development was the public forum it gave the workers, and the opportunity for debate and possible organization. I came home all excited and Dan and I talked until 1:00 a.m.

The next day I went to see Sr. Brito and we discussed the cooperative idea at length. His reaction was a negative one, as he cited the laziness of the men and their penchant for politics, but he did admit there are promising aspects. He agreed to a ceramics painting course and even said the mayor's office would have money to spend for a tourist brochure. Dan came to town then and we went to talk to Zezenia, one of the leading ceramics workers, who also feared the cooperative wouldn't work at that time but was willing to participate and help motivate others. I wrote up a plan, but it still needed to be fleshed out.

I later resolved a few things with a visit to LBA and learned they wouldn't fund cooperatives anymore and hadn't done so since 1964 when the military took over the country.

Journal entry, February 17–It's been a marvelous, soul-searching week for me. First, getting all excited about the idea of a cooperative for ceramics workers, then pretty much giving up the idea as impossible but rushing around to get the project for a painting and glazing course turned in. Then there was a meeting Friday for organization of a mother's club. There's also the library project, the garden project, and the health campaign to think about.

Sometimes I feel like I'm in a trash can and

someone's trying to stuff me in by pushing on my head with the lid. Why am I trying so hard to do so much? Why do I get so many ideas and persist in carrying them out? Am I humanitarian or am I trying to make these people think I'm a saint? Am I trying to build up a good record or score Brownie points? If so, for whom? Why can't I be content to do a little good instead of a lot? What will I do if I can't be helping someone or trying to improve things? Why can't I mind my own business and do just enough to pass inspection? And will I admit that there is something beyond my powers? What if I tried something and failed? I have to be a reformer. A crusader. No wonder I'm a nervous wreck. No wonder people feel uncomfortable around me and say how inferior I make them feel. Will I ever change?

All my life I've been trying to impress people, probably mostly my mother. The only person I don't feel like I have to impress is my husband. That's probably my salvation. He doesn't expect a fraction of what I expect of myself. What will I do when we get home where the place is full of overachievers? I think I'm unhappy here in Brazil, but it could happen that this will be the only place I'll ever be happy.

Our Peace Corps friend David said I would die early, probably with ulcers. Admittedly, I am still nervous, yet much less so than two years ago. I still overreact to everything and expect too much of others. I expect them to conform to my ideas, my standards. Maybe the first thing I should work on is controlling my emotions, my reactions to people and events, by keeping them more to myself, and thinking before spouting off.

Now that I know what's wrong with me, I don't feel any better.

The meeting we scheduled with the ceramics workers was

really frustrating. We gave them so many ideas on how to improve their sales and production, but they seemed stuck in their traditions. The only thing they decided was to ask the mayor to reopen the ceramics museum. Otherwise, they weren't willing to work together for the good of all.

-21-

GOOD DAYS AND BAD DAYS

Zenilda and Glaucidete finally got paid for two months of teaching, except that it fell short about 40 cruzeiros of what they were promised. They began talking about quitting, so it was up to me to convince Sr. Brito to pay them what they deserved. If he refused, there wasn't much use of the school continuing, or even of thinking about staying in Brazil any longer.

If the town couldn't afford to pay two girls 40 more cruzeiros a month when they'd studied for their diplomas four years, then there weren't conditions to maintain a school. They only agreed to teach with the understanding that they'd receive a higher salary than the other teachers who weren't *formadas* (graduated from a teacher training). Besides which, they had to pay transportation amounting to 40 cruzeiros. If they left, it would disrupt the school tremendously. They'd been trained for this type of work, they were good with the children, and the children were used to them.

Besides that sticky business, we were looking forward to *Carnaval* and reserved a table at the club in Carpina. The kids in the school would be having their own *Carnaval* party, complete with horns, streamers, drums, tambourines, and masks. Then classes would not be in session all the following week. The girls needed a break, and so did I. By the end of the holiday, I intended to buy materials and plan cooking and sewing classes and try to find the mistake in my last quarter bookkeeping.

We got good news in the mail the week before *Carnaval*. Dan's draft induction had been cancelled, and he would be reclassified 1H. We could start planning our lives without worrying about another two to four years in the army. We discussed what we wanted to do once we got home to stay, including moving back to Columbia to work and study. We definitely wanted to go back to Missouri. Dan liked being in the country and we both looked forward to being near our families. I had just thought the other day how great it would be to, say, go to a play in Kansas City with Mother—just the two of us on the town, enjoying ourselves and getting reacquainted. Two years before, I never would have thought about doing that. But being so far away from her gave me a different perspective on our complicated relationship.

Our complex mother-daughter issues were later spotlighted when our volunteer friend Suzanne admitted I made her uncomfortable any time she was at our house, because I made her feel like she should be doing something. I guess subconsciously that's the impression I was trying to make. Mother always made me feel like that, banging around in the kitchen until I felt obligated to help her.

By mid-March I went to Recife to get in touch with a Professor Baldini about teaching the ceramics course but had no luck finding him. Then I ended up at Mercado San José looking for yarn and checking some prices. I bought a mosquito net for 68 cruzeiros, and hoped it would help us get some decent sleep without hearing buzzing around our ears and waking up with bites.

That's the trip to Recife during which I had a traumatic dentist visit. The anesthetic didn't take effect completely and I almost kept my mouth shut tight to try to keep the drill and the pain away. Then I cried. And I still had to go back two more times.

I think the tension in my personal relationships must have extended to my work relationships as well. One day I blew my top when Zenilda said she wasn't going to do anything with the kids for São João festivities and Dezinha said she was going to look for a new job when I left. Then Zenilda admitted she enjoyed seeing me mad.

Maybe I wouldn't have reacted so strongly if the school didn't mean so much. But when I thought about it, why should I care if Zenilda doesn't do a square dance this year? It won't hurt me. And if Dezinha does go work somewhere else, it's not as if she's abandoning me. That's the way I reacted, though, taking things way too personally. I vowed to change my ways.

Plans for the school construction continued in March. On the 20th I went to the center and got Sr. Brito to go with us to measure the land for the school. We then went together to Nazaré to prepare the deed for the school land but ran into complications. The owner of the land where the new school was to be built owed money to the government and couldn't even give away any of his land because of indebtedness. Sr. Brito made plans to go to the federal land office to see if he could expropriate the land without a clear title. If everything went well, we'd be able to clear the land in at least two weeks.

We also decided to ask Sister Maria José, the head of the Tracunhaem parochial school, for the use of the land by her school for our center's vegetable garden. We tested the water pressure there to see if it would reach inside the wall for watering the garden, and it did. Sister Maria José promised to take the case for the garden to her Mother Superior.

Sr. Brito and I also discussed a library project. He agreed to hire a librarian and furnish a building for the library.

On my trips to Recife I began dropping in to visit the officials at LBA, making friends and networking with Georgette, Fernanda, and Helvêcio as I tried to appropriate the money for building the grade school. Helvêcio asked for 5,000 cruzeiros for our ceramics course instead of the 10,000 I asked for. That was the second time that had happened to me. However, he did have an instructor who could be interested in teaching our course.

On that trip to Recife, we ate a big lunch with fellow volunteer Marian at the Chinese restaurant and later had a banana split. I bought some material to make embroidered placemats then went to the Peace Corps office to help with some office filing. We had a *Malôte do Cabo* afterwards then went to the Chinese restaurant again for supper. Trips to restaurants were always a delightful activity for all of us.

The Portuguese translation for diplomatic pouch is *Malôte do Cabo*. The translation for *Cabo* is less exact and more mysterious, as it means Cape.

Almost every week a diplomatic pouch arrived in Recife from our national Peace Corps office in Rio de Janeiro. There may have been an American consulate involved in placing some of the items into that padlocked leather pouch. I can't recall if that's how we got our monthly living allowances but that sounds right. There may have been medications for the volunteers and there were definitely items of correspondence between the various Peace Corps offices, from Washington, to Rio, to Recife.

It doesn't really matter all that much what was in the pouch, but rather what occurred after its arrival. Inventive volunteers used the arrival of the pouch as a cause for celebration; specifically, a big, drunken party in the back yard of the office. In retrospect, I wonder how the neighborhood put up with hearing music and loud voices until the wee hours.

The big Peace Corps office parties occurred even when there was no *Malôte do Cabo* arrival, such as when a long-time employee was retiring or when a Peace Corps couple or trainers got married or left for the States.

As had been my custom since childhood, I didn't really get into heavy partying or drinking. I just quietly observed all the revelry, since I didn't like beer, and often just tried to engage in a quiet conversation off in a corner. Seldom did I allow myself the luxury of losing control by drinking to excess. It was more fun to watch everyone else.

Then came the day that rated as a minus five on a scale of plus ten. In the middle of all the good days I'd had for two weeks, Sister Maria José sent word to me that we could have a little piece of land next to the school for our garden, but the rest would stay as-is. That didn't bother me so much. But then she said she didn't want to participate in the clubs, after we'd already enrolled the mothers and girls. She had seemed so excited before this. It was a low blow and I reacted in typical Anne mode, becoming depressed and melancholy.

I wrote the following letter to her but don't think I ever mailed it. It illustrated the sensitive maneuverings and diplomacy that we often had to employ, always with the risk of committing an unintentional insult:

Dear Sister Maria José,

I hope this letter finds you happy and with good health.

I am writing to you because at times it's very difficult for a foreigner like me to explain myself, and because I'm a journalist, I feel better writing.

I became very sad to know that you do not want to participate any longer in the clubs for mothers and girls. For me it was a big surprise because before this you seemed so enthusiastic.

I did not want to make more work for you. On the contrary, I wanted to help your work, giving some financial assistance. I know that sisters have lives full of hard work and poverty and with the assistance I have received from LBA, our club would have been a really big thing. It wasn't going to be necessary for you to come to the meetings more than one time per week. And it would be the mothers who are going to do the majority of the work in teaching the courses, planning the meetings, and in the end, that is what our goal was. You would not have been the coordinator or even the responsible person. In terms of the mothers who are teaching for free, I had already thought about giving them a small stipend from the money that has been allocated for the clubs each month.

I was led to believe that your club had been suffering from extra expenses and lower participation. Forgive me if that impression was in error.

If everything goes well, Nininha is going to take my place, and since she loves to work so hard, I believe she would have provided an enormous collaboration to your club.

In the end, we decided to continue our clubs as well as yours. I could not disappoint 68 mothers and girls who have already enrolled. I did not anticipate any of these 68 women that have enrolled leaving your club and I know many of them are already used to you and others don't care for the Americana.

And now, the subject of the garden. I'm not going to need the piece of land that adjoins the motherhouse. We did a school garden project that gave us a lot of produce for the children of Tracunhaem. If the garden were larger, there would have been enough vegetables to provide more nutrition than the macaxeira and mango that the mother house receives from time to time.

Forgive me if it appeared that I had my eyes on your land. We just didn't have another place large enough and I didn't know if the mayor's office would be able to buy land near the new center. And you know that it is difficult sometimes to secure these things from Sr. Brito. At times it takes a person like me, an outsider, to arrange for them more easily. The mayor's office had already resolved to put a water spigot inside your wall since water was not already in your school plot. It would have helped a lot.

I came to Brazil, Sister, to work for the good of the community, to promote cooperation and action between all. I don't work for personal gain. It is true that I don't lack for anything in life but instead I work for the pleasure of it and to see progress in a city that is sad from poverty and ignorance. It was not easy to leave my family and friends, but the joy of seeing these children learning and their parents wishing to raise their standard of living has already paid me for any tears and homesickness I might be feeling for my own country.

If anyone here is under the impression that I am trying to take control of everything, then I am to blame. I love to see cooperation, and in the fight to secure this perhaps I stepped on the feet of some or meddled in a place where I should not have. It wasn't intentional.

Since arriving in this town, I had three dreams in addition to building a new pre-school: to start a library, start mothers and girls' clubs, and make a school garden. I cannot work alone. The school garden will not happen now. And in the mothers and girls clubs it appears we cannot count on your help. The library ... we will wait and see.

I had never been content to build only a pre-school. I guess I have the sickness of the young—impatience and a desire to do big things. Forgive me for these faults that may have caused you difficulties.

I remain your American friend,

Ana

-22-

WAITING FOR GOATS

Marian, an older, single volunteer we had trained with, was known by her fellow Americans as the goat lady. She had been a goat rancher in California before joining the Peace Corps and her goal for her site in rural Pernambuco was to bring a pair of purebred goats from the States and introduce superior genetics into the nearby herds. This was the kind of program the national Peace Corps office got excited about because it represented the trend for planning more scientific and business-based projects in all countries, but especially Brazil.

The pending arrival of the purebred goat couple was cause for high anticipation in the Recife Peace Corps office and in the country where they would be made available to local farmers for breeding with their goats.

With our journalism backgrounds, Dan and I had been assigned to document the goats' arrival and do a feature story to send to the Peace Corps headquarters in Washington.

On April 3, we got up at 5:30 a.m. and Dan and Marian went to the airport to wait for the goats. I went to catch a bus for Carpina in time to oversee another vaccine campaign. Just like the campaign we held at Tamataupe, the administration of vaccines at Trachunhaem was chaotic.

Toward the end of the day, Dan called and left a message at the mayor's office and said he couldn't come home. One of the goats had kidded in the Rio airport, so they couldn't send them to Recife yet.

I kept pretty busy at the center the next day but had to borrow 50 cruzeiros from Sr. Brito to pay the center's light bill so they wouldn't cut the power off (and we didn't even get a bill).

In cooking class that day we made fruit salad, *doce de batata* (sweet potato dessert) and *sonhos* (a light, fried pastry).

After class, Dan called again and wanted me to take a bus to Recife, but it was too late. The goats still hadn't come, so Dan took the last bus out and after supper we rented a car to go back to Recife.

I worked at the Peace Corps office that next morning on files and typing purchase orders but the goats still hadn't come when I left after lunch to go back to work. Only 16 mothers showed up for Mother's Club but we had a good meeting anyway. We elected officers and they signed up for courses. I even got them to sing a song at the end.

Dan came home at 9. The goats finally came in! The next day he read all day and tried to recuperate from Goat Week.

We were awakened that morning by someone clapping at our gate. It was a guy named John, a cultural geographer and Fulbright Scholar who was doing a nutrition study. He was living in Buenos Aires, Argentina and came to record prices at the local farmers market, had breakfast with us, and we talked until 10. Then we went over to Bob and Karen's for a scrumptious Sunday dinner. Afterwards, Karen and I took the Jeep to the supermarket where I shopped for the school while the guys went to watch the soccer game on TV.

The next day we took the supplies over to the school and I went to talk to the woman who's going to teach sewing classes. She also offered to teach flower making and silk screening. That afternoon was the first Girls Club meeting and they seemed to really enjoy themselves.

I took the bus out of Trachunhaem after the end of the meeting and went straight to Recife all the way, still hearing in my head the strains of the girls singing "Young World." The theater has good acoustics, and they sounded great.

Dan came in soon after I did, and we took a taxi to the Recife seminary to meet the new Peace Corps volunteers who were in training. After a light supper, some of them went to a nearby bar for a few hours. The volunteers were all in the office the next morning for orientation and we had been assigned to help with that too. They were sure paranoid about their health and nearly ran the medical supplies inventory out of paregoric and insect repellent. Dan ran around all afternoon doing things for a sick volunteer while I typed and filed.

Back at work the next day, I caught an early bus to Nazaré to get 1,000 cruzeiros out of the bank, and had an interesting conversation with the bishop and Sister Rita about torture, censorship, etc. They seemed so hungry for any stories I'd heard. I repeated a story I'd heard about Dom Helder Camara trying to buy land and about an American priest who was in prison for four months of interrogation. The religious in Brazil have fewer restrictions than average citizens, but they still got in trouble. Stories of imprisonments often circulated between priests and nuns who had first or second-hand information. They were always seeking confirmation from anyone who might have some details, including a mostly-clueless American.

Back in Trachunhaem I went to look at the school progress and saw workers had covered the well and were plastering inside walls.

The next day Dan and I took the Jeep to Recife, and I went to LBA to turn in my trimester report. While there I talked to Helvécio, who said he'd worked with volunteers before and was impressed with our idealism and dedication. He also admitted to feeling frustrated by his work in LBA.

This seems to be a good week for heavy conversations. Just the day before, I had a long talk with Donna Noemia about her unsolvable problem—their inability to have children.

I was meeting so many frustrated people and my heart ached for them. Dona Noemia says I'm too sensitive, too empathetic. But that's probably the way I'll always be. I like to feel life while I'm living it. I'm just not looking forward to the suffering that everyone tells me I'm in for.

Our staff meeting later that week became a little heated. Glaucidete and Zenilda got into it over São João festivities and the fact that someone told Ninha that Zenilda would leave when she took over from me. What a mess! Everybody left depressed and mad.

And Dan was traveling all over to put together a slide show program for health volunteers, so I couldn't even dump my worries on him.

Journal Entry, April 22, Easter Sunday—For the second day in a row, we awakened to a steady rain and leaden skies. It's really been a lazy, peaceful two days, but I like the sunshine better. I was so happy to see Dan after he was gone for two weeks. I don't think he liked being away so long. But the tour of health programs he took was enlightening. He brought back some semi-precious stones from Minas Gerais—a hematite, an aquamarine, and two peridots. He also bought a tapestry hammock in Fortaleza.

The last two weeks I have felt like I was in limbo. Everything stopped while Dan was gone. Now hopefully time will move forward again. We both have lots to do. I imagine the cooperative will have lots of things for Dan to do, and I've got mountains of activities with the center. Mother's Day is coming up and the kids will start rehearsing in late May for the Feast of Sao João. My cooking and sewing classes are going well and there's the construction of the new center to think about, as well as the grade school.

The days in April became a blur of daily trips to Trachunhaem or Recife for me and Limoeiro or Recife for Dan. I worked my butt off at the Peace Corps office on the files in the reference library and took an inventory of the medical cabinet. I'm not sure why I felt compelled to do it. I didn't even take a lunch hour. But they had asked me to help out when we returned from our leave and they knew how my Virgo self just loved organizing and feeling useful.

Helvécio had good news for me in April, informing me that he had secured someone to teach the ceramics course in Trachunhaem.

On a trip that week to Nazaré to see the bishop and get more operations money, we almost got into a discussion of modernism versus traditionalism in the church, but we were interrupted. That could have been interesting.

People mobbed me as soon as I arrived at the school. The women were there for painting class. Sr. Brito came by, and we resolved a few things about the construction, then went to the building site to agree on the height of the exterior wall. We also went to look at some mosaic tiles to put on the floor.

That afternoon was a girl's club meeting. All went smoothly but I had such a cold and sore throat it was hard to talk. They got a kick out of the talk I gave on menstruation *faz mals* (taboos). And they really paid attention to the drawings of the reproductive organs.

I felt rotten by the time I got home. Dan fixed supper and I worked on a translation for his health slide show.

Journal entry, April 25–Finha Nova cried again this morning about our leaving. I felt like crying too. As I listen to Brazilian music, I get that heavy feeling in my chest that has nothing to do with this cold.

Not many months ago I was crying in frustration and loneliness and wishing we were at home, and now I can't bear the thought of leaving. These next few months are going to be crammed full of activities and things that make memories.

That last party with the kids during the Feast of São João is going to be really something. And of course, there's the inauguration of the new building to look forward to.

The girls in the club are already wondering why they didn't get to know me sooner. I could kick myself for not organizing these clubs sooner, but these things must go slowly. The time was ripe only now.

Dan brought home a letter from his sister Cathy. I

guess I haven't forgotten about home, as happy as I was to hear news from there.

-23-

GYM CLASSES, MOTHER'S DAY, AND A FUND RAISING FEIJOADA

As our time in Northeast Brazil began winding down, our schedule of activities ramped up exponentially. One memorable activity was a girls club hike to an abandoned country church. It was a wonderful trip and the weather perfect. The walking wasn't bad until we started climbing the serra. Then it was steep, at least for me. One of the girls carried my bag.

It was so peaceful up there. The girls climbed trees and took naps on the church sidewalk. I talked to Nininha for hours and we saw three marmosets, two snakes, and a tarantula. Nina and Socorro were seen leaving in a car with two boys. The other girls were indignant, and I talked to them about being non-judgmental. Toward the end, we sang songs and had an informal talk about friendship, then played games. The walk back seemed much longer than the walk there. I went to bed at 8:00 and was sore all over.

I was still sore for our first gym class. Why on earth I ever agreed to lead that activity I'll never know. But there were several girls in attendance, and we had a large audience. We had them do jumping jacks, leg swings, running in place, touch toes, and then tested their motor coordination with a jump rope and bouncing a ball. They weren't as bad as I expected. We had relay races with the balls and then they ran laps. It was fun.

The next day I went to Recife to take in some film to be developed, check prices on volleyball and ping pong sets, buy a whistle for gym classes, material for the girls' uniforms and some for myself too.

While we were there, Delano (one of our original trainers) and Kathy had a party at the Peace Corps office to celebrate their marriage. Lots of people attended and they finished off a pony keg of beer before 11. José, the long-time Brazilian custodian/driver for the Peace Corps office and a good friend of Dan's, went around the party crowd carrying a tea kettle for serving beer and saying "Tea. Tea of India." What a character!

On May 8 the mother's club had their Mother's Day party. They planned it all themselves and did all the work. It was nice, but they all cried. In fact, that's the main reason they attended. The concept of motherhood in Brazil was best summed up by the phrase I saw on so many posters: Motherhood is pain and suffering.

The mothers and children who attended a Mother's Day program at the Tracunhaem theater.

I think they take to heart the religious teachings about the suffering of Mother Mary, and the cultural norms here that leave women powerless to do much but lament their condition.

As I arrived at Trachunhaem for work on May 22, the first thing I got hit with was the disappearance of 36 cruzeiros from the money I'd left for emergencies. But I glossed over the issue and went to talk to Sr. Brito and we went to the construction site to agree on some of the details. That afternoon we had a directors meeting and decided to have a *feijoada* (bean feed) to earn money for the construction.

Feijoada is Brazil's national dish, but it's also a party, a celebration. The black bean and meat stew is rich in blended flavors and almost always accompanied by unique side dishes that include farofa, rice, orange slices, and sauteed collard greens.

During the World Cup, or anytime there is a soccer team playing, families gather to prepare and later to indulge in this comfort food meal. Baptisms, confirmations, anniversaries, and birthday parties all seem to call for a *feijoada* celebration. And even though I had a disdain for beans and rice, my favorite way to cook back then and today is to throw a bunch of ingredients into one pot and let the flavors simmer into richness.

And while I cooked mainly the American dishes I longed for while living in Brazil, throughout the years we spent in Pernambuco, I developed a fondness for many of the flavors of the country. I am a total cilantro freak, and I love to chop and mix it with a fresh tomato pico de gallo. I know. That's actually Mexican, but Brazilians had something similar but without the jalapeños.

Early in our training, I loved sitting down to a meal with Brazilians who knew how to make a rice dish with a cream sauce, onions and peas, topped with a layer of melted cheese. I would make it often when we returned to the States.

In the meat department, I struggled with cooking Brazilian grass-fed beef. It was so tough, and I don't think we had a pressure cooker. Poor Brazilians didn't eat much meat and got their complete protein by combining rice and beans. If they were lucky, they had a scrap of pork fat to throw into the bean pot to flavor it. They frequently ate sun dried, salted beef called *carne do sol* (meat of the sun). The closer they lived to the coast, the easier it was to purchase fresh fish on the beach, sometimes right off the little fishing rafts that returned from their daily trips beyond the reefs.

While we were in Brazil, we had the advantage of being more mobile than the people we worked with and got to travel all over the country during those three-plus years. On one of our trips to Rio de Janeiro, we were treated to a Brazilian barbecue at a churrascaria in Petropolis, a city high up in the cool hills above Rio. That's where we had our first experience with skewers of various meats being brought around to our table as waiters sliced chicken, beef steaks, sausages, shrimp, and fish onto our plates. At a Brazilian barbecue, it wasn't even all about the meat. There were a staggering number of filling side dishes of vegetables, potatoes, and rice.

I was elated a few years ago to enjoy a Brazilian *churrascaria* in Kansas City. It brought floods of *saudade* or homesickness washing over me, similar to what happens when I overhear rare but serendipitous snatches of Portuguese in public.

I probably wasn't indoctrinated sufficiently into Brazilian cuisine when we decided to have a *feijoada* to raise funds for the school construction, but I pushed ahead with plans, certain we could pull it off as easily as all the other events and meals we had organized. That was a mistake.

I wish we had used this recipe that I found online a few weeks ago on seriouseats.com.

Brazilian Feijoada

Ingredients

- 1 pound dried black beans, picked over
- Kosher salt
- 1pound salted pig parts-ears, trotters, salted pork fatback, slab bacon (see note), cut into 1/2 to 1-inch pieces, rinsed of excess salt
- 1 pound linguiça, longaniza, or South American chorizo (or a mix), cut into 1/2-inch thick slices
- ½ pound carne do sol or corned beef, cut into 1/2 to 1-inch chunks (optional)
- 1 large onion, diced fine
- 1 green bell pepper, core and seeds discarded, diced fine
- 6 scallions, white and light green parts only, sliced fine
- ½ cup chopped fresh cilantro leaves
- 1 large tomato, finely diced

- 3 bay leaves

To Serve:

- Cooked rice
- Orange wedges
- Sautéed kale or shredded cabbage
- Hot sauce
- Farofa (see note)

Directions

1. Dissolve 1/4 cup kosher salt in a gallon of cold water. Add the beans and allow to soak overnight (at least 8 hours). Drain and rinse.

2. Combine soaked beans, pork parts, sausage, beef, onion, pepper, scallion, cilantro, tomato, and bay leaves in a large saucepot. Cover with water by 2 inches. Bring to a boil over high heat. Reduce to a simmer and cook, topping up with water as necessary to keep beans completely submerged until beans are completely tender and liquid is a deep black, about 6 to 8 hours. Season to taste with salt (you probably won't need any more, depending on how salty your pig parts were). Serve with rice, orange wedges, greens, hot sauce, and farofa. Feijoada is excellent reheated.

Notes

For best results, use as many different salted pork parts as available, though you can always make it with just a few. Straight up salt pork and slab bacon with some good sausage will be quite delicious.

Farofa is fried manioc (yucca) flour. It can be found in Brazilian markets ready-to-eat, or make it yourself by toasted rough-ground yucca flour in a bit of oil in a skillet over medium heat until golden brown.

FEIJOADA FAILURE, PORNOGRAPHIC SONGS, AND RELATIONSHIP BREAKDOWNS

The bean feed was held June 9 and was a total flop, despite our intense preparations. I shopped for ingredients with Dezinha. I had tickets printed, and transported food from the market to Trachunhaem to cook at the school kitchen in the same big pots that the kids ate their lunches from.

The problem was the beans did not soak long enough. And we didn't allow ourselves enough time to cook them after they soaked. They were crunchy beans. And boy, did those who paid to eat the dish complain! Finally, the American had a failed event. For several days I didn't want to show my face in public and face my detractors and critics.

That failure seemed to even lead to a string of other mishaps and relationship challenges. Some were minor, but others seemed major. The worst one was dealing with an incident where a young man named Chegue was overheard singing a pornographic song about me. Everyone thought I should complain at the police station and teach him a lesson. So, I did.

The only witness we could find was Gil, Dezinha's son. The rest of the guys who heard Chegue singing the song would not admit it, but they put him in jail anyway for five hours to set an example. Meanwhile, Dezinha had a nervous breakdown, screaming and crying and tearing at her clothes. She was so ashamed that she had to go to the police station with Gil.

I think everyone around me was just plain stressed that things would be changing when we left to go back to the States. Zenilda, ever the ornery manipulator, started arguments every chance she got. One day she told me she was taking the new records I bought home with her. I asked why and she said to rehearse the *quadrilha* (Brazilian square dance) at her other school. I must have given her a dirty look because when she got in the car, she said, "I didn't take your records." Then she told Glaucidete she'd better come and rehearse the quadrilha because she wasn't going to.

Zenilda got mad at Finha for throwing some syrup and an aspirin in the trash. Finha cried, Zenilda thought she was being a baby and said she'd never feel the same toward Finha. She probably felt the same about me.

On occasion during that time of trial, I got to the center depressed and down for some reason, and they hit me at the door with all kinds of problems. The biggest was a broken sink. I went to see Sr. Brito, and boy was he sharp with me! I don't know if he was mad about something or just having a bad day himself.

The women's club had a crafts exposition toward the end of June and all of us just wanted to get it over with. It didn't go over very well, and no one sold any of their crafts. I ended up buying all of the brilliantly colored needlepoint pillows the women had made and treasure them to this day when I see them scattered on the arm of a fainting couch in our family room.

Despite the trials and conflicts during those last months of work, there were bright spots and accomplishments. I was doing a few things well and correctly.

Journal Entry, June 5–Sometimes I seriously doubt that my techniques are working, that doing things in meetings and through group discussion is perhaps not the thing to introduce into a culture without such a tradition. But something happened today to encourage me.

The president of the Mother's Club came to set up a meeting of the officers and she thanked me for the orientation I gave. She said she's been elected to so many offices, but never has anyone told her what to do, and never has she participated in meetings where everything hasn't already been decided beforehand.

Sometimes I think I'm trying to push them into things too soon, without ample preparation. But I told Elizabeth to observe how I held a meeting so that next time she could do the same. And Neta is really getting the hang of the accounting, which she will be taking over when I leave.

For the Feast of São João that year, I got ambitious about Brazilian cooking and made *canjica*, a traditional corn pudding with coconut milk and topped with cinnamon. We had a hard time lighting the bonfire, as it had been so wet. Each year during that holiday everyone lit a bonfire at their front gate to invite good luck and prosperity into their homes. Even though it took awhile to light, that last bonfire brought us good fortune and better luck than the hectic, conflict-ridden months that preceded it.

-25-

WRAPPING THINGS UP
WITH PARTIES

For our last July 4 holiday in Brazil, the girls club took a trip to Vicencia and climbed another mountainous hill. I almost didn't make it, as my fat and blue jeans slowed me down. In the evening, we had homemade ice cream at our Mennonite volunteer friends' house.

A few days later Dan and I held a big party in the back yard of our house. Despite the rain, it was a success. For once, instead of stressing about the house being clean and all the food being planned and perfect, I didn't get nervous and actually enjoyed myself. We all danced, and our Peace Corps bosses and trainers came, along with all the Mennonite volunteers. I played the flute and someone played Dan's guitar. We had lots of leftover food but the brownies disappeared quickly. I worried at the time that one of our enterprising Peace Corps friends might have laced them with marijuana. They had done that at a previous party at a volunteer's apartment in Natal. It was the first time I had ever been exposed to wacky weed, and the only effect it had on me was to make me hungry. But it scared me out of my mind. I was so afraid we would get caught and end up in a Brazilian prison.

In those dwindling days of our Peace Corps service, Dan and I had become heavily involved in national and regional volunteer programming. Dan traveled all over the country taking photos and putting together a slide show for health care volunteers who would be entering training. I wrote and illustrated a recruitment brochure and traveled to Rio in August to oversee its printing.

175

The front cover of the Peace Corps-Brazil recruitment
brochure I designed and wrote.

Despite our many activities, they didn't keep me busy enough
to stop worrying that I wasn't doing things right.

*Journal entry, July 15– I cannot get my mind to work
right. It's all in a jumble. If I let myself, I could get nervous
and uptight. As it is, I'm scatterbrained and can't
remember anything long enough to get it down on a list.
I'll probably forget what I did with the list anyway. I'm
just bothered. Bothered about Trachunhaem, about how
Sr. Brito doesn't want to build the grade school and
doesn't seem to want to put Nininha in my place. I'm
bothered about how the mothers and girls' clubs are
functioning so precariously. Bothered about who's going
to replace Glaucidete and if Sr. Brito will want to name
some fool featherhead. I'm half-blind right now and can
only see the problems, the obstacles. The successes and
accomplishments seem dim in the back of my mind. Will I
get it all together?*

We always seemed to find time to go on weekend trips and enjoyed another one to Natal, but without the marijuana brownies for dessert.

On July 23 we spent the morning on the beach, ate a fantastic lunch, and toured Radio Northeast. That afternoon, Howard, the Rand Corporation guy we had for a trainer when we first got to Brazil, gave me a test on attitudes toward work and toward subordinates. It turned out that my primary work style consisted of a high concern for task and a high concern for people, with backup styles of high concern for people and moderate for task. But I felt that was my style when working with Brazilians. I hoped to keep it, as it produces best results in work situations. Later that evening, we had a big discussion about sex, inhibitions, etc. I stayed out of it and tried to read the book that got the discussion started.

We flew back from Natal on the Bandeirante, a small Brazilian airline named after an outlaw, and I got out to Trachunhaem in time for the girl's club meeting. I gave a talk on reproduction, and they were all open-mouthed at the illustrations. They also had many questions, and I learned they really didn't have much of an idea about sex or having babies. Their mothers have admitted to me they don't know much either. They just remember their husbands coming home drunk and all of a sudden, they're pregnant. I knew better than to ever talk to them about birth control in this country of Catholics. Especially when I'm working with nuns and a bishop.

Later that week I went to Recife to work on the office accounting and in the afternoon went downtown to buy tennis shoes for some of the kids and for some reason started looking at material. I spent almost 200 cruzeiros and had a designer draw two outfits for me to travel home in. Then I chastised myself for losing my good sense. But it was fun to splurge and do something I hadn't planned on once in a while.

In Trachunhem the next day, I talked at length with Sr. Brito and learned we wouldn't be building the grade school in addition to the new pre-school. That was quite a relief, for some reason. At least it was one less responsibility. Brito told me that some chief came from Brasilia to visit the construction site, and he seemed satisfied with what he saw. He had come with Helvécio from LBA, and they walked around town talking to people. Helvécio told Brito that the money had been released and for me to go to LBA as soon as possible to sign papers to transfer funds to the bank in Nazaré.

In the days that followed, things got back into some semblance of routine. The kids came back to class and I spent most of the day getting organized and talking to the girls about how things are going to change at the center, with more economy, etc.

On July 30 I went back to Recife, talked with Georgete about the center and Helvécio about the ceramics course. The first course would begin around the first of September. Dan and José and I had lunch at the Doctor's Club and then came out to Carpina. They went on to Limoeiro to take pictures and go fishing.

We had a good staff meeting on July 30. I was able to stand up to Zenilda and wasn't afraid of her when she said she didn't want to march in the center's inauguration parade. She always had a way of cowing me. But because I was firm, I didn't lose her friendship. In fact, I think I earned her respect. She didn't really mean half of the things she said. I finally figured out she says them to show off and hide her true feelings.

As our work began to wind down, I kept busy at home in the evenings packing things to ship home and bringing clothing and household items to Trachunhaem to sell, donating the proceeds to the building fund.

The new center construction was almost complete, and we began to decorate the interior classroom space, paint and arrange new furniture.

By August 19, Dan and I took a trip to Rio to oversee the printing of the recruitment brochure, enjoying some down time by going shopping, and to see the movie *Serpico*. Before leaving, I dropped by the Recife Peace Corps office to pick up the results of a recent stool exam and discovered I had giardia. Good ole protozoa. What a great exit-from-Brazil gift. No wonder I hadn't been feeling very well.

While in Rio waiting for the brochure proofs, we took a quick bus trip to Belo Horizonte to talk to the new health training group. On August 23, we flew back to Rio, made a quick trip to Copacabana to buy a new purse and eat a horrid lunch at Gordman's, then went over the first proofs for the brochure. Dan recorded his slide show script at the American Consulate, played volleyball at the Peace Corps office, then we left for the bus station. It was a nice trip back on the *leito* bus to Recife and I enjoyed a long, leisurely read of *Sybil*.

Once back at work, my journal entries reflected the squeezing of time into many last-minute activities and celebrations.

August 25–Where did August go? We got back from Rio this morning at about 9:00 a.m., relaxed and rested all day. I wrote a letter to Mother, and we looked through some travel brochures on South America.

August 26– It was a pleasant day at work, and everyone seemed so happy to see me. It's obvious they're planning something for tomorrow. The kids marched for the first time today, rehearsing for the inauguration. What a mess!

August 27– Today was one of the nicest birthdays I've ever had, in Brazil or in the States. This morning at the meeting of recreation leaders, Georgette recognized me and my birthday, saying all kinds of nice things. They gave me a book on children. Even Doctor Edesio, the top chief of LBA, wished me Happy Birthday.

That afternoon there was another party at Trachunhaem. When we entered the Cine Teatro, everyone was there—kids, mothers, girls. Glaucidete led us down the aisle and the kids threw rose petals on me. Two boys recited poems about me and one of the girls spoke on behalf of the Girl's Club. I received a nice gift from everybody, a slacks outfit. They had a big cake and other goodies and even gave me flowers. They sang songs, one of them with improvised lyrics:

"September already comes. Aunt Anne is already going away."

Sr. Baé played Happy Birthday on his ukulele.

The only thing keeping it from being a perfect day was the case of feverish diarrhea I had that evening.

August 28–The Girl's Club meeting was successful. I used some of the group dynamics techniques on them and they thought it was the best meeting they'd had. I wish I'd known how to use these techniques a year ago.

I got a letter from my mom today.

August 29– Just like the nicest birthday, this turned out to be the nicest anniversary we've had so far in four years. In the morning, we went to Recife to LBA for the meeting for directors, and once again Georgete recognized my work in Trachunhaem.

In the afternoon I went shopping for material for the school kids new uniforms and bought Dan a travel kit. Bought myself one, too, and got back to the office with a mountain of packages, and Dan had already gone home. I was furious, but when I got home, I found him in the kitchen fixing an anniversary supper with candles on the table. We had fried shrimp and onion rings, tossed salad, and a fruit cocktail with whipped cream for dessert.

August 30–I went to Nazaré to plan the field trip for Sunday. Later at the school I tried to get myself organized but it didn't work. I can't keep my mind on the school. It keeps drifting to traveling home and packing.

The cooking class prepared a really good luncheon. Only two kids showed up for class, so we sent them home.

September 12– *I'm so tired and nervous thinking about all the stuff I have to do before we leave. I don't feel right about taking time away from the school to go to a party, and especially to go to Fernando de Noronha the weekend after next. I'm leaving all the details of moving until the last minute. By the end of the month, I should be a psychological wreck. I would like to go to sleep and upon waking find that someone has taken care of all the details.*

September 24–I must be more nervous than I realize. I'm losing weight, my lips are chapped, and I'm constantly tired. Today was hectic, but no different from the last two weeks or more. I really needed to go to Recife but went to Trachunhaem to plan the inauguration with Sr. Brito. I tried on the skirt and vest Aziza is making for me and then looked at the clay statues that Nielsen made in the afternoon. We'll be sending them back to the States in a big sea crate Dan is having made.

I took an inventory of kitchen supplies and talked some to Nininha. Finally, I went to look at the kiln we've purchased for the ceramics class, then spent most of the evening marking prices on things to sell.

AN INAUGURATION AND A NERVOUS BREAKDOWN

I don't remember much about the inauguration of the new pre-school. I do recall the children marched through the streets of Trachunhaem waving small Brazilian flags. I remember the Bishop wore his priest's white robe over his black clerical garb as he blessed the center, sprinkling holy water at the entrance.

The Bishop of Nazare da Mata, my project supervisor, officially inaugurated the new pre-school.

183

The children marched in a parade through the streets,
led by teachers Glaucidete and Zenlida.

Although it was not intentional, my clothing complemented the priestly garb. I wore the outfit Aziza made for me. I wish I still had that black and white skirt and vest with a black blouse, beautifully embroidered on the puffy sleeves with white thread.

Several dignitaries attended the inauguration, driving in from Recife—officials from LBA, Peace Corps directors, and some volunteer friends. Sr. Brito was front and center to unveil the plaque that listed the people behind the building, including Dan and me.

Inside the new building, all was perfection, or so it seemed to me. The rooms were painted in beautiful tropical hues and stenciled letters proclaimed that this was *"Meu Recanto,"* (my corner). Zenilda and Glaucidete had painted and cut out large images of Donald Duck, Mickey and Minnie Mouse to decorate the walls. The child-sized furniture was freshly painted, the toys in place, and craft supplies ready to be used by the children.

Zenilda (left) and Glaucidete were teachers in the pre-school. For years after we left Brazil, I wrote letters to both of them at least once a year.

The city flag of Tracunhaem covered the dedication plaque at the new pre-school and was removed during the inauguration by Mayor Sr. Brito.

In the director's office of the new building three large, framed photographs hung on the wall—the President of Brazil, the Governor of Pernambuco, and me.

We had done it.

And now I was leaving a piece of myself behind– largely my heart and love for these children, the staff members, the mothers and girls from the clubs. I could only hope it would remain a school for a long time, and that Nininha would find satisfaction and joy in taking my place as the center's director.

But I didn't realize until a few weeks after the inauguration that I was not at all ready to leave my home in Brazil.

We had liquidated all our household belongings, selling them or giving them away to friends. One of the last items to sell was a large box fan, which Sr. Brito claimed for his wife.

In just a few days we would be leaving Pernambuco and saying goodbye to our wonderful home in Carpina. We had already said our farewells to our jobs and the people we worked with. I made one last trip to Tracunhaem to settle a few last-minute details with Nininha. We were talking on the veranda of the school, resting our forearms on the exterior wall, when Sr. Brito pulled up in front of the building. He opened the back door to his car and pulled out the fan he had bought and said, "We decided we don't need this after all. Could I have our money back?"

I looked at him with shock on my face, protested weakly, but dug in my purse for the few cruzeiros he had paid for the fan and watched him get back in his vehicle and leave. Then I lost it.

"What am I going to do with this," I wailed to Nininha. "Why did he bring it back? I don't have anywhere to put it. We're leaving in a few days and won't be back. I can't put this fan in our luggage and haul it across Brazil and South America!"

The full weight of our uncertain future suddenly punched me in the gut. I began sobbing hysterically and could not catch my breath. My chest hurt. It felt like I was having a heart attack.

Why did the mayor's parting gesture make me feel like he'd slapped me in the face? Did he blame us for going back to the States and leaving the running of the school in the hands of Nininha? Was he saying, "Good riddance?" Did he not realize how much this complicated my departure? Or so I thought at the time. I was not using reason at all and certainly making a mountain out of a molehill.

From the safety of years of coming to terms with my dysfunctional past and my insecurities, I now know it wasn't about the fan. It wasn't even about Sr. Brito. Neither was it about any failures in my work in Trachunhaem or even about my inability to control what happened to the school or the students in the future.

Instead, that fan had everything to do with my feelings of insecurity at not having my next year mapped out for me. Not having goals or a to-do list other than preparing for a three-month long trip back to the States. Not knowing where we would live or what we would find to do with ourselves after being Peace Corps volunteers for more than three years.

I didn't recognize any of that in my encounter with a returned fan, at least not while I was fighting to bring air into my lungs in between hysterical hiccups.

Nininha saw the color drain from my face and led me quickly into the school office and told me to sit down on the floor with my head resting on my knees. She went into the kitchen to retrieve a teaspoon of sugar, which she mixed in a glass of water and ordered me to drink it. In about 15 minutes the sugar water mixture calmed me down enough that I could walk to the bus stop, head down in embarrassment at my tear-stained face and my inability to control my emotions. I apologized profusely to Nininha for being such a crybaby. What a way to leave. What a horrible last impression of immaturity.

As I boarded the bus for my last 15-minute ride to Carpina, I felt as if I'd been swimming in the ocean, unable to resist a strong undertow that was sure to drown me. When I got home, my entire body ached with fatigue and trembled uncontrollably. I could barely speak when Dan met me at the door. But he listened patiently and sympathized with my ordeal. Neither of us had the background or experience to name my experience as a panic attack. Meltdown wasn't even in our vocabulary back then.

Journal Entry–Saturday, October 5, 1974 - *We are*

finally almost free of ties in Brazil and beginning to feel a stronger pull toward home. The next three months is going to be a much-needed transition period between two distinct cultures, sets of problems, responsibilities, etc. It would have been so much better leaving Brazil without the run-in with Sr. Brito. I keep dwelling on it, and every time I find myself thinking about it, I tense up. He didn't deserve all this mental anguish that I've been directing at him. Thank God he didn't even realize how it affected me, unless Nininha told him about it. All I hope is that the school remains open. It's time to stop worrying about things I have no control over.

That includes mother's impending divorce. My stepfather had gone to work at the Sirloin Stockade in Bolivar, Missouri and started having an affair with a woman just a few years older than me and left Mother to go live with her.

After talking to Mother on the phone last night, my mind isn't eased at all. She can't pull herself together and can't understand why, after so many hardships, she can't cope with this one. I think I know why. She's 42 and never in her life has she felt secure or felt that she could lean back and rest and have someone to depend on. It's been one constant struggle after another. Unfortunately, she can't lean on her children. I hope she finds someone or digs up the self-reliance to start all over again.

It's so nice today. The first chance I've had to rest in two weeks. And what do I do? Mend. Play the flute and write. We spent the morning on the beach. There's something about the wind and the waves that smooths out the wrinkles and renews a person. There is so much of nature and raw force that it overwhelms and numbs and drives away heavy thoughts. I hope this trip back to the States and an unknown home is restful and fun. I can't let it be ruined by worrying about the future.

TAKING THE LONG WAY HOME –
A NARRATIVE POEM

We sold our stuff, packed souvenirs in a sea crate, and parted company with Brazil. As soul separation hit, pain reigned. I gasped for air, hiccupped in sobs. What would we do now without a sense of purpose and belonging? Well, we could start an adventure, taking the long way home, meandering down the coast, launching out from São Paulo into the interior where Spanish is spoken instead of Portuguese. We dangled our arms out wood windows as our train chuffed its way through endless jungle, halting inside the Bolivian border to wait out another of their military coups, already so travel weary we weren't alarmed by soldiers crouching behind mounds of dirt, practicing enemy maneuvers by pointing their rifles at us. Brazil homesick and homeless, we hopped a cargo train for Santa Cruz, choked down coal dust and empanadas before jumping on a plane to Cochabamba, then on to La Paz for a dose of altitude sickness. We took a taxi to Puno, leaving in the cold with a cold, only to get carsick on the altiplano. We bought train tickets to Machu Picchu at the Indian market in Cuzco, the odor from urine streams pooling around the feet of the multi-skirted women wearing white hats intensifying the ache of being estranged. We piled into VW buses for a hair-raising ride up hairpin-turn switchbacks to a seven-wonder site, scrambled over rocks of ruins, sat on a king's throne, and fell under the spell of a long-gone civilization. Later, in Lima, we stalled for weeks in gray pollution and melancholy waiting for a wire transfer to finance continued travels. On the long way home, we tasted ceviche, stumbled onto a bullfight, and dug for clams in the Caribbean. We ate huevos rancheros in Chichicastenango, rode in the jump seat of a bus all the way to Panama, toured a museum of erotica in Mexico City until the day we stopped, settled stomachs and stifled *saudades do Brasil*, to fix our eyes on formerly familiar snowy horizons. Still, I could feel Brazil's sea breezes caressing my cheeks, the sand of its beautiful beaches pushing up between my toes and into the part of my heart I left behind.

EPILOGUE

My eyes have been opened so much lately by working on and researching my time in the Peace Corps. My journals from those days have given me a look at my attitudes as a young woman—my often selfish, arrogant attitude—and how it was shaped by my environment, by what I was reading and even by the music of the era. My generation was so counter-cultural, so "entitled" and so spoiled (some of us anyway).

We were influenced by the women's liberation movement, the Civil Rights Movement, the Vietnam war and campus protests. But looking back on my attitudes and my complete buy-in to notions advocated by writers like Dr. Joyce Brothers to always "put yourself first," I am appalled at myself. How could I have been so self-seeking, so intent on achieving my goals for my own self-esteem and self-fulfillment? And why could I not at least release my heart and pour out my soul to God, since I could not do so fully with my husband back then?

How many people did I wound in the process of maturing into myself? How many people suffered their own lack of self-esteem by my arrogant commitment to tasks? How many people did I cause to feel "less-than" by re-doing what they did, just as my mother did to me?

A few years ago, when I drove by the house in Grandview, Missouri where my family lived when I went to high school, it seemed so much smaller than the house of my memories. Today I found just the opposite in a virtual visit to Northeast Brazil.

The world has become so much smaller now when you can type

a far-flung location into a search bar and instantly pull up images and videos of that place. When I entered names of places we lived in Brazil 53 years ago, I discovered it had grown larger and prospered. I watched YouTube and Facebook videos and drone footage of the places I called home back then until I developed vertigo and had to stop.

The only place I spotted anything familiar in the videos was Engenho Tamataupe de Flores. But the virtual visit there was a haunting one. The landscape captured by tourists with smartphone videos and Portuguese commentaries has changed dramatically since the mid-1970s. Or maybe my memories are faulty. The veritable ocean of sugar cane was gone, replaced by open spaces for grazing cattle. Most of the lush, ancient trees had been cut down, probably for firewood or fuel for cooking stoves. But new owners have no doubt recognized the historic value of the place because the video claimed it was one of the most important, intact sites for economic development and history in the state of Pernambuco. The place now shows signs that tourists are regular visitors, complete with metal barricades to keep them from entering the private family areas.

The smokestack from the old sugar mill still stood in the center of livestock barns and corrals. All the buildings had been recently whitewashed, and a large, hand-painted sign now proclaims the name of the place. I even spied electric transmission lines coming into the *engenho* to replace the generators we once relied on. I spotted the pond we walked around every day. The road into the plantation remains unpaved—dusty in the dry season and probably still next to impassable in the rainy time.

The old church is still there and sports a fresh coat of paint, but its massive doors appear locked tight and inaccessible to visitors. The structure housing the side altar has disappeared. No doubt it crumbled into the clay ground around the caving-in crypts beneath the table the school children and I sat at when it functioned so briefly as a pre-school.

I wish I could have spotted something familiar in the virtual tours of Carpina and Trachunhaem. Carpina has become a bustling metropolis with a rush hour and many modern storefronts. Trachunhaem, where we attempted to organize the ceremics workers, is now an arts mecca. Large clay statues line the sidewalks of the main street into town, and an impressive arts building functions as the nucleus of a weekly artisan fair. I'd like to think I helped plant the seeds that sprouted so much progress and development, but that's probably a stretch.

I so wish I could go back to Brazil to scope things out in person.

But my passport expired a few years ago, and since I have had two knee replacements, these old legs are probably not spry enough for overseas travel.

We did make a trip back with Dan's parents five years after leaving Brazil. And Dan returned in the late 1990s with his new wife. (Yes, we divorced in the mid-1990s when our son was six years old, and he remarried shortly afterwards. But that's another book. Or not.) They visited Trachunhaem and ran into one of the cooks for the school, Finha Nova. She brought them into her home where they spotted a photo of me on the wall above a kind of homemade altar. Hearing that truly humbled me and at the same time it verified that at least one person I knew from our Peace Corps days had looked into my heart and knew I had come to Brazil to love and to serve, even as I sought self-esteem. It also verified that my photo was no longer on the wall at the pre-school. But why would it be?

I won't ever see Finha Nova's altar to my younger self. She's long gone by now. And while I recently discovered Glaucidete and Zenilda on Facebook and reached out to them, they probably thought I was an American hacker and didn't respond. I have a new last name and my profile photo doesn't much resemble my 20-something photos.

Instead of renewing acquaintance with my long-lost foreign home, I will content myself with old photo albums and memories of a time lived far from the broken homes of my youth. I will dwell on the good times, the friends, the beauty of the land and its people, and feel immense gratitude. I have forgiven myself for being so clueless, so intense and driven, even as I recognize some of the same habits of work, over-achieving and list-making I first adopted as a Peace Corps volunteer.

I'm so grateful my experiences in Brazil set me on a path that led to a purpose I pursue even now in my old age—learning something new each day and then sharing it with anyone who cares to listen.

THANKS FOR HELPING HANDS
AND BOOK MIDWIVES

I have birthed many books in my career, but none have presented with more childbirth pangs than this one. Maybe that's because it took 50 plus years to get it out of my heart and onto the page. And it wouldn't have happened even then without some friends to coach me through the process.

Thanks to my son, Michael Chadwick, for pleading with me to write this story, and then not accepting my first draft of transcribed journal entries. You can do better, Mom, he said. Cheri and Craig Battrick had the same comments when they read that first draft in 2018.

The biggest debt of gratitude I owe to my good friend and fellow book publisher, Thea Rademacher of Flint Hills Publishing. She offered to publish it for me instead of my having to push it through my own book publishing firm, Personal Chapters. Thea also held my hand through all the stages of imposter syndrome and my whining about who in the world would even want to read this story that happened so long ago.

My husband, Wayne, has always been patient with my long hours closeted away in my upstairs office, writing or working on client books, but with this book he had some interrupted sleep. Insomnia drew me to the computer during the wee hours to revise and put the finishing touches on it. I promise to pay more attention to keeping the house a bit more presentable and fixing meals in a timelier manner. I'd like to promise to resign from so many outside volunteer obligations, but this habit started in Brazil so it's not likely to change. Sorry, dear.

A big thanks to every one of my advance readers, blurb writers, and launch team. While I had long advocated for my own book clients to form a team prior to their book launch, this is the first time I've practiced what I preached.

Finally, I have so much gratitude for the giver of any inherent talent and creativity I possess–our Creator. The Universe's back up choir includes all my guides and angels and deceased relatives who form an invisible but felt team to cheer me to the finish line.

OTHER BOOKS BY ANNE SPRY

Living on Laughter: A Memoir of a Former Humor Columnist and Newspaper Publisher by Anne Spry

Riding Rainbows Through the Storms: Finding Perspective and Hope by Journaling Through a Pandemic

Finally Noticing: Poems and Photos Prompted by a Pandemic

Journaling with Jesus: Writing to Heal from Trauma–A Masterclass by Cheri Battrick and Anne Spry

Searching for Summer: A Solved but Unresolved Missing Persons Case (co-authored with Brandy Shipp Rogge)

Rebuilding Your Life After the Death of Your Spouse: Experiences and Tips from Two Survivors by Anne Tezon & Craig Battrick

Tripping Down Main Street: The Fun and Funny of Community Journalism

Letters from Home: A Newspaper Column and a Memoir

ABOUT THE AUTHOR

After living in South America as a young woman, Anne Spry spent a lifetime seeking a stable home, mostly in Missouri. She put her journalism degree from the University of Missouri to work in a 27-year career as a newspaper editor and publisher in Hamilton. During that time, she also earned a master's degree in communication arts from Memphis State University. Instead of landing her a job as an instructor at her alma mater, like she hoped it would, the degree pushed her into working on book publishing even while running her newspaper. Once she sold the paper and moved to Kansas City, book publishing became her retirement avocation.

Destined for another move when her second husband died, Spry was blessed to go back to her roots and settle on ancestral land a few miles from where her parents grew up. She lives on five acres with incredible views of spacious Kansas skies, plants flowers, sings with a Sweet Adelines chorus in Topeka and is active in Kansas Authors Club.

Anne is married to Wayne, a retired military pilot. They enjoy spending time with Wayne's three children, grandchildren and great-grandchildren and sharing good times with Anne's three young grandchildren.

www.personalchapterspublishing.com

www.ingramcontent.com/pod-product-compliance
Lightning Source LLC
Chambersburg PA
CBHW031507120626
46545CB00005B/1782